W9-ANM-800

FRANCES WILLARD
of Evanston

When I reach heaven, I want
to register as from Evanston.
F. E. W.

Statue in the Capitol, Washington, D.C.
(dedicated in 1905)

FRANCES WILLARD

of Evanston

LYDIA JONES TROWBRIDGE

WILLETT, CLARK & COMPANY

CHICAGO NEW YORK

1938

Manufactured in The U. S. A. by The Plimpton Press
Norwood, Mass.-La Porte, Ind.

To My Parents

William and Mary Jones, who with the Willards constituted a mutual admiration society

Contents

Foreword

"WRITE US THE STORY OF YOUR LIFE," BEGGED HER FRIENDS, "to celebrate your fiftieth birthday. A true story, not one that through conventional modesty omits half the truth."

From that voluminous autobiography, which she called *Glimpses of Fifty Years,* and from many other sources, one who loved her in life has compiled a story that seeks to be equally truthful, interpreting little, appraising not at all, letting facts speak for themselves. Enough that Frances Willard fought valiantly for the right as God gave her to see the right, fought with faith in him and in the ultimate coming of what she liked to call "the Republic of God."

Introduction

OLD EXETER HALL WAS CROWDED. FIVE THOUSAND BRITISH men and women sat with eyes fixed on the platform as notables filed in: members of Parliament, London county councilors, church dignitaries, labor leaders, temperance leaders, and delegates from fifty guilds, leagues and other societies. Last of all, two women: Lady Henry Somerset and Frances Willard.

For them the audience rose en masse, waved handkerchiefs and gave three lusty cheers.

Lady Henry, heir to an earldom, voiced Old England's welcome to a daughter of New England, whose name was a household word among workers for reforms throughout Great Britain.

A frail, gentle woman rose to reply. Could this be the famous organizer and leader of thousands of women the world over? Incredible! But as she talked, her whimsical blend of wit and wisdom, her challenge to the foes of society, her augury of victory captivated her listeners. They, too, caught visions of a far-off utopia.

Yet why all this adulation? After all, what was Frances Willard but another agitator for teetotalism?

To think of her as only that misses the real significance of her life. True, she preached total abstinence and the abolition of saloons by state decree. But she preached also the ballot for women, their equal opportunity and responsibility in the home, in professions, in industry, and in affairs of state.

She *preached* these, but she *talked* about many other reforms. Some of them the world is still merely talking about. Foremost was education for citizenship; a close second was physical education and sports. No one was more insistent than Frances Willard on vocational training for girls, on equal pay for equal work, on a minimum wage and an eight-hour day. She was an early advocate of international brotherhood and compulsory arbitration of industrial disputes, and of a democracy that would ignore differences of race, class and creed. She talked; what is more, she won thousands to her way of thinking. Few have been more successful in molding public opinion.

Seven years she worked actively with and for a political party founded by what she called "political philosophers." Others called them "cranks." Yet at least ten of the planks first shaped for their platforms have since become laws of the land.

She was a Methodist, but a Methodist of today rather than of her own day. Anyone the wide world over might work with her for social betterment. Hers was a religion of action. It was this that caused the throng in Exeter Hall to rise and cheer at sight of her. It was nothing she had said, nothing she believed; it was that her words and beliefs had been transmuted into action. She had started reforms in forty spheres of public welfare — in America, in Europe and in Asia.

Through the magnetism of love she had reclaimed thousands for their homes and for society. For the love she gave, love flowed back to her. Ten years before the tribute was paid to Jane Addams, Frances Willard was called "the best-loved woman in America."

FRANCES WILLARD
of Evanston

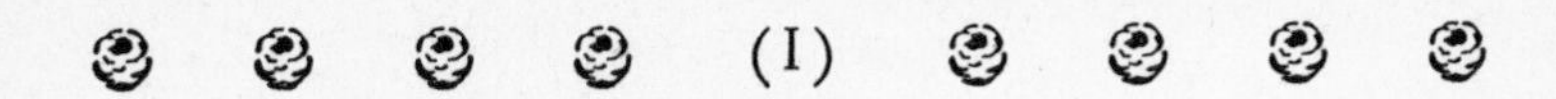

(I)

Welcome Child

FRANCES ELIZABETH WILLARD WAS BORN IN CHURCHVILLE, New York, the twenty-eighth day of September, 1839. Her mother had been a teacher; her father was manager of a store. But when Frank — as they called her — was two, her parents came to a great decision, hastened, perhaps, by the panic of 1837. Josiah Willard and Mary, his wife, were no longer young; she was thirty-nine and he a little older. Still they longed for more education. Josiah thought he had heard the call to preach; Mary meant to keep pace with him. Only Oberlin among colleges admitted both men and women. They would go there. And go they did — driving by carriage all the way. Sarah Hill, Mary's sister, went with them. Oliver, aged seven, sat beside his father; Mary, Sarah and little Frank occupied the back seat.

It was a wearisome five-day journey. More than once the baby wailed, "Mamma, Sissy's dress aches!" And the mother said happily, "Dear child! She already knows it isn't her real self that suffers, but this dress of mortality!"

In time the child once Churchville's "doll baby" came to understand why her mother called her "welcome child." She was no dearer than sturdy Oliver, but two baby girls before her had "gone back to God," and Mary Willard wanted a daughter. The baby was welcome to Josiah, too, though sometimes when he was walking the floor to still her lusty cries he would say, "This young one ought to amount to something; she gives trouble enough!" At forty the cares of fatherhood weigh a bit heavily, especially with a bottle baby at night.

In Oberlin Josiah bought ground and built himself a home, which he landscaped beautifully. Five years passed like most years, with alternating light and shadow. Much of the light radiated from a new baby, named Mary for her mother. But the shadows lengthened as ill health grew upon Josiah and he came to realize that the ministry was not for him. " An outdoor life," counseled his physician.

Three pictures have been preserved from that period. One is of little Frank gazing fascinated at President Finney of Oberlin as he preached. The flash of his eyes beneath white lashes and the deep roll of his voice were like lightning and thunder. She snuggled closer to her mother. Another is of the child lifted to look on a corpse in its " chilly shroud," and shrinking back as if struck a blow. The third is of the child standing erect on the gatepost, mimicking the gestures and voice of a student " orating " for her amusement.

Baby Mary was less independent, more cuddling than her sister. She called out all the tenderness in her undemonstrative parents. But between the mother and her " welcome child " existed a depth of understanding nothing could disturb. For more than fifty years it was Frances Willard's anchor.

An outdoor life — what could that mean but life on a farm? So Josiah and Oliver (now twelve) fitted out two prairie schooners with billowing canvas tops for their household goods, and made ready to move still farther west. The first wagon was driven by a student who had joined them; Mr. Willard and Oliver drove the second; Mrs. Willard, the girls and a woman companion rode in the carriage drawn by the family horse. At the tail of the procession trotted their big Newfoundland dog. Sarah Hill remained in Oberlin.

To Mary Thompson Willard, who at forty aspired to further

culture and education, life on a farm in what was still pioneer country meant the burial of all her aspirations. How could she know that that farm would be the making of at least one of her children? Or was it she, the mother, who in her wisdom was to use the farm as a tool to mold that character?

Day after day for three weeks the procession trekked steadily westward, except on the Sabbath. Josiah took his time, stopping along the way to make inquiries about farmlands. He knew land values. For more than two centuries most of his relatives had been farmers. At last, in Wisconsin, on a bluff overlooking Rock river, he and Mary found the site they fancied. There he pitched a tent and began building.

The children reveled in this outdoor life. For Mrs. Willard, tenderly reared, accustomed to comforts and conveniences in a staid community, roughing it must have come hard. But she bore this, as she did all hardships, with fortitude and serenity. If in afteryears the young Willards were proud of their mother's resourcefulness she could credit some of it to those days of camping. Said she, "We carried all we had learned with us and gave it to our children."

In time Forest Home, the "Willard place," came to be recognized as one of the finest stock farms in a state already noted for its dairies. Willard cattle walked off with blue ribbons enough to prove their quality.

"Come, come!" someone will say. "Where did Josiah Willard get the money to do all this?" It had certainly taken money to finance a family of five during those years at Oberlin. It took money now to buy a farm, even though virgin soil and small at first; to build a house, though but one room and an attic. It took money later to raise blue-ribbon stock and "as many as a thousand" sheep. By that time the farm maintained two tenants. Where the money came from is not told. Josiah's father had been a well-to-do farmer in Ogden, New York, and Josiah had by his " ability and dependability " risen from clerk to manager of a store. Occasional glimpses of relatives on both sides of the family show them prosperous — people from whom their pioneering brother or " in-law " might have borrowed. Josiah demonstrated his genius for farming; such men have little difficulty in securing bank loans. Whatever he turned his hand to prospered.

Mrs. Minerva Brace Norton, a cousin of Josiah's, finds it hard to restrain her admiration. " His uprightness, intelligence, interest in politics and practical affairs," she says, " together with a certain personal magnetism, made him easily a leader. He became recognized as an authority on agriculture and horticulture. His reaper was the first in that area, and passers-by stopped to watch him, his two little girls squeezed in beside him, his son standing back-to-back raking off."

He rose from plain " Mister " to " Squire " and then to a seat in the state legislature, carrying with it the title " Honorable." Yet he seems to have treated all honors casually, as matters of course in the life of a man whom God had given the wit to serve himself and his country.

During their first two years on the farm Josiah and Mary Willard were busy preparing a home. Oliver helped his father in the fields and with the stock; the girls cared for their increasing family of pets — " live dolls," Frank called them in afteryears. For Frank's seventh birthday busy Mrs. Willard made a big rag doll, with real curls saved from some earlier day; Mr. Willard painted its face, " with the most surprising pair of eyes," says his daughter, " it has ever been my lot to see." Fifty years later the memory of that great day was distinct: " Doll Anna was attired in a turkey-red calico gown made from one of mother's old aprons, and I was permitted to hold her all day, except when I put her to sleep on mother's high four-posted bed. The birthday cake was not forgotten, though farm work was pressing. Greatest honor of all was permission to wear mother's gold pencil all day."

Mary loved to help around the house. Frank disliked housework; she preferred carpentry and gardening, making her own tools from old boards and scrap iron. In their sports she led, being the older by four years. Since they had no toys the girls invented sports. Sometimes they rode on the beam of Oliver's breaking-plow, three times the size of other plows; sometimes they mounted the horses that pulled the cultivator; sometimes they hung bags of corn, beans, onions, or seed around their waists and helped Oliver plant. If there was a prairie fire they beat out stray sparks, while the men dug a trench for backfire or carried pails of water.

Oliver must have been an extraordinary boy. Though five years older than Frank and eight or nine years older than Mary, he joined heartily in their sports. Always he was their pattern; it was the height of their ambition to take part in *his* sports, whether marbles, tops, quoits, stilts or prisoner's base. Four of his pastimes were, however, forbidden them: hunting, swimming, boating, and horseback riding. Swimming and boating remained on the forbidden list (as too dangerous on the river, perhaps) but in time the girls were given guns and horses. The ban on riding Frank had especially resented, since her mother had been a fine horsewoman in her youth. Not to be outdone, she trained her heifer Dime — first to be led, then to be curried, then to pull a sled. But when it came to being saddled Dime stood on her rights as a cow; many a tumble did Frank have before her father, pleased at her persistence, gave her a horse.

As a woman, Frances Willard pleaded for the children who had no vent for their ingenuity, whose lives were hemmed in

by people. In childhood she had seldom seen people outside her own family. Animals had been her intimate friends. Her world she had made for herself.

It is evident that Frank's was a healthy childhood. "Mother's Rules" were the law of the land; no one dreamed of questioning them. They were simple rules: plain food, plenty of outdoor exercise, no tea or coffee for the children, no alcoholic drink for anyone. Last rule of all: "Tell the truth and mind your parents." The parents never expected their offspring to be bad. Frank and Mary and Oliver enjoyed outdoor life and plenty of sleep; as for alcoholic drinks, they had never seen any, much less tasted them. When neighbors came to help thrash they praised Mrs. Willard's nonalcoholic "harvest drink." From her favorite book, *The Slave's Friend,* Frank came to know that Negroes were not the only slaves; strong drink had its slaves also. But the question did not touch her directly. Josiah Willard was a total abstainer, and his membership certificate from the Washingtonian (temperance) Society hung on the dining-room wall.

One day Frank found a pledge in her Sunday school paper and asked permission to paste it in the big family Bible for all the family to sign. The pledge and its signatures would be no ornament to the expensive book, but the older Willards rarely objected to their children's plans. There the pledge stands today, duly signed, with Oliver's two crosses to indicate that he reserved the right to drink beer and cider. It reads:

"A pledge we make no wine to take,
Nor brandy red that turns the head,
Nor fiery rum that ruins home,
Nor brewer's beer, for that we fear;
And cider, too, will never do.

To quench our thirst we'll always bring
Cold water from the well or spring.
So here we pledge perpetual hate
To all that can intoxicate."

Having observed this ceremony, temperance was forgotten for years by all of them, except Oliver in college.

Forest Home was several years abuilding — "a queer old cottage with rambling roof, gables, dormer windows and little porches, crannies and out-of-the-way nooks scattered here and there." Little is said about the interior, save that it was built around the dining-room. Only "Father's Room" is described in detail, the one place where silence was imposed, though the children could come and go, and play there when they pleased. Its most distinguished piece of furniture was the tall secretary. No one but the "Squire" ever sat at the desk. In his absence it was locked. But the bookcase above was always unfastened. From it the children drew freely. By the time she was fifteen Frank had read all of Shakespeare and many of the classics.

It was not the house, however, but the outdoors that delighted the young Willards — "the river flowing broad and free; the prairie stretching away to meet the horizon; fields yellow with grain in summer, fleecy with snow in winter; groves of oak and hickory on either side. In the pasture was heard the cow-bell's merry tinkle, blackbirds in the poplar grove, complaint of the mourning dove, sweetest and saddest of songs." Around the house was "a miniature forest of evergreens; . . . vines winding around pillars and over windows; thick shrubbery and the perfume of flowers." Further off was the pets' graveyard, each grave sodded and marked with a white shingle on which was inscribed a childish tribute to the dear departed, such as, "Beauty and Brighty, our pet rabbits. We loved them but they died."

Never was Frank to forget "the witchery of springtime" on the farm, when "dear old Mother Nature whispered secrets she did not tell to most folks."

The family rose at dawn in summer, long before dawn in winter. Squire Willard seated himself at his desk; Oliver and the hired man went to milk the cows and feed the horses; Frank and Mary looked after their pets — turkeys, chickens, peafowls; rabbits, goats, calves, colts and dogs. In the kitchen Mrs. Willard and Bridget got breakfast.

Sundays were different. Josiah Willard was — in those days at least — a seventeenth century Puritan. Beyond providing food for the animals and the family he permitted no work to be done on Sunday. He did not shave, nor did he black his boots; he did not write letters or even look up a word in the dictionary. Yet he was not stern or harsh.

Church services were infrequent. The Methodist minister was on a "circuit," visiting each church in rotation. When there was a service the family, including the help, dressed in their best and clambered into the farm wagon (the carriage is no longer mentioned) for the four-mile drive. As prairie fires became more frequent one of the family remained at home on guard; the parents and Oliver took turns. They seem to have been equally good cooks; the family dinner never suffered. No one would have thought of asking Bridget to curtail her day of rest.

On churchless mornings Mr. Willard whistled to the sheep-dogs, and squire, girls, and dogs strolled to the river at the foot of the high bluff. Oliver lay face down on the porch, his nose in a book; near him Mrs. Willard in the rocking chair serenely read her Bible. At the river Frank would now and then surreptitiously skip a stone, being "something of an adept" at that. She would have liked to cut whistles out of willow twigs, but her father ruled that whittling was carpentry and not to be done on the Sabbath. Whereupon Frank gained one of her earliest victories by compromise. Might she whittle if she did not make anything? Her father assented.

Sunday afternoons the girls went with their mother to the orchard, Mrs. Willard's special domain. Here they learned the ways of birds and plants and of the little creatures that scampered about among the trees. Here their mother quoted her favorite poets — Coleridge, Cowper, Thomson, Addison. Always, when twinkling stars came out, Frank was to remember Addison's poem beginning:

"The spacious firmament on high,
With all the blue ethereal sky
And spangled heavens, a shining frame,
Their Great Original proclaim."

Sunday evenings were given over to singing around the melodeon, "sometimes thirty songs one after the other." Frank and Mary took turns as accompanist. They feasted on poetry and song. Even their daily dozen — which they called "calisthenics" — were done to a missionary hymn:

"Bounding billow, cease thy motion,
Bear me not so swiftly o'er!
Cease thy motion, foaming ocean,
I will tempt thy rage no more."

What matter that to them the lines were meaningless? There was the rhythm of little arms and legs — up, down; forward, back; bodies bending, necks twisting. Religion permeated even their sports.

There was something rare about Mrs. Willard. She came to be called "Saint Courageous," for she accepted life as unquestioningly as she did her husband's decisions. But both were sweetened by her tact and her resourcefulness. She did not "bombard heaven" with her prayers, but took God's love for granted. As for Mr. Willard's decisions, her methods of getting him to modify them were cleverly adopted by her elder daughter, as in the case of the whittling. Mary wore down opposition by teasing; Frank gained what she could by compromise. She confided to her journal that, if she couldn't be a saint — and she knew she couldn't — she would like to be a politician. Unwittingly she played politics from her earliest years.

In those days Christmas was but a popish holiday; New Year's was the day of gifts. Once, when New Year's fell on Sunday, the gifts were distributed Saturday night, to avoid breaking the Sabbath. To Mary and Oliver went books; to Frank a long-wished-for slate. On Sunday Mary and Oliver could enjoy their presents, the books being religious. But poor Frank couldn't use her slate, since drawing would be "making something." In desperation she appealed to her mother. Couldn't she draw, if she made nothing but meetinghouses? Yes, said Mrs. Willard firmly; and, to forestall any objection on her husband's part, she drew the first meetinghouse as a pattern.

On the whole, Frank did not mind the Sunday prohibitions much. What she did object to was "talking religion." She says, "My faith faculty was not strong." When at six she was told that the Bible was God's message to us she asked, "How do you know?" Fortunately neither parent talked religion much; they lived it. So Frank was left to think out life's mysteries "with sighs in my little breast." Family prayers did not interest her; Sunday school lessons she straightway forgot; but she liked to memorize from the Bible. *Myrtle* (for little ones) and later the *Sunday-School Advocate* furnished fresh reading matter not too religious in character. Her favorite books were *The Slave's Friend* and *The Children's Pilgrim's Progress*. The former early implanted in her a sense of universal brotherhood and a desire to help the weak. The latter — "sweetest book of my childhood" — gave her in Greatheart her first hero.

From the time when she stood on the gatepost imitating student orators or was set on a chair by her father to say her piece, she delighted in "speaking pieces." At ten her favorite was Campbell's description of the fall of Poland. She could never repeat the last line — "And Freedom shrieked when Kosciusko fell" — without a quaver in her voice and tears in her eyes for the great patriot gone down to defeat. Patriotism was half her religion.

Meanwhile her parents, whose first desire was that their children be Christians, watched and waited and prayed.

(II)

Growing a Soul

FIRST RELIGION, THEN EDUCATION, SAID THE PARENTS. FOR TWO years, however, there was no formal schooling at Forest Home. School, as the Willards knew, is only a part of education, often a small part. They did not regret having to turn their children over to Mother Nature, best teacher of all for those who will give heed. Oliver at twelve, Frank at seven, Mary at four became well acquainted with all the creatures that flew or burrowed or ran in fields and woods; they knew when and where to find each wild flower, the names of trees and their habits, the names of rocks and pebbles, and why the bluffs along the river had taken on queer shapes. In a word, they learned at first hand — with the help of their parents — the elements of zoology, botany and geology. They sketched nature, too, in their self-taught way.

Though they did not go to school, there was a " night school " in the vine-clad cottage. As his flocks and herds increased in size and quality, " Squire " Willard took on more farm hands and installed Bridget in the kitchen to relieve his wife — whom, by the way, he always called " Mrs. Willard " as she in turn called him " Mr. Willard." Whether Swedish, Norwegian or German, most of the hired men were green immigrants who needed to learn to read and write English in order to become good citizens of their adopted country. Miss Willard gives us a glimpse of the help gathered around the dining-room table, learning the three R's and the Constitution of the United States, while she, a nine-year-old, sat making " pothooks." One evening she said suddenly, handing her mother a sheet of foolscap, "Just write my name for me in your nice hand, and see if I can't imitate it pretty well." Thus she began to write.

That winter Mr. Willard entered the legislature, for Wisconsin was coming into statehood. Week ends at home he was more than busy planning the farm work for the following week. Frank's desire to write, however, pointed out to him a new duty — to "arrange" for a schoolroom. Just how much labor he was at to arrange it we are not told. Perhaps he added another room to the cottage — a mere trifle to this capable man. In his carpenter shop he made four desks and four benches; for the Willard girls were to be joined by the two Inman girls, the neighbor's daughters. The four were to be taught by Mrs. Willard and Oliver. This arrangement continued three years.

Meanwhile the children were transforming the farm into a world of their own. When a "girl" from Janesville complained of the loneliness of the country, Frank retorted: "Well, if we ought to have a city here, we'll have one. A town of our own. You townspeople depend on others for your good times; we have to depend on ourselves." Her father agreeing, she and Mary set to work.

The farm was christened Fort City. The farm buildings were renamed: the barn became Mr. Willard's Warehouse; the well, City Fountain; the pigpen, the Stockyards; the cowyard, City Market; the henhouse, Mrs. Willard's Supply House; the granary, the City Elevator. There were a bank, a board of trade, and a newspaper office where the *Fort City Tribune* was printed on Oliver's hand press. The city charter made provision for five officials, the tax gatherer not being forgotten. As the city was to be "a place where everyone can live happily," saloon and billiard hall were prohibited. "No saloon, no jail," said the young founders. Frank was to live to see her ideal realized in the prohibition state of Kansas — where there was " no poorhouse either."

Since civilized man cannot live without money, even in Fort City, the children cut silver coins from tin and gold coins from yellow leather, and Mary cut bank notes from paper and decorated them. Last of all came a good-roads campaign, when the children filled in and leveled the farm roads, and named them Broadway, Market street, and so on.

The " Squire " had his sanctum; his elder daughter must have hers. She established it in the crotch of a burr oak, installed a box for her books, and named the place " Eagle's Nest." The box served also as a desk on which to write editorials for the *Fort City Tribune*.

Frank organized the Artists' Club for sketching tours, when Mary's goat carried in its panniers the artists' sketching materials and lunch. There was also the Rustic Club for hunting, organized when their father gave them rifles. The children made their own hunting suits of calfskin and boots of cowhide.

Whatever the organization, it had its rules and regulations and demanded parliamentary procedure. That was the way Frank's mind worked.

In all these activities the parents worked quietly behind the scenes. The laws might be childish, but the phraseology was legal. Mrs. Willard was justice of the peace; all disputes were brought before her. Mr. Willard helped make sleds and tools, bows and arrows, wooden bowie knives and guns — everything that could be made of wood, leather or metal. He made paper hats, which Mary decorated with feathers and drawings.

Frank was twelve when the Fort City Board of Education was created, " Mrs. Willard in the chair." Oliver, now seventeen, had become a " Janesvillean," and every day he walked six miles to town and six miles home to attend the Janesville Academy. But he entered heartily into the game with a long, grandiloquent speech, ending: "Frank and Mary ought now to have advantages greater than it is possible for you, Mrs. Chairman, in the limited time at your disposal, to bestow upon them. So I move that we found an academy for their special benefit." They formed themselves into a committee of the whole and delegated Mrs. Willard to interview the Burdicks, lately come from New York City to settle across the river. Shortly thereafter Miss Annie Burdick came to live with the Willards during the summers and teach the girls.

Miss Burdick was inspiring. She taught the girls to analyze flowers; she gave them plenty of poetry. Frank liked the poetry especially. One can imagine her riding furiously through Fort City in imitation of Cowper's John Gilpin, or delighting a Friday afternoon audience of four parents with "Alexander Selkirk" delivered in her best style. Miss Burdick encouraged the girls to write. She taught them geography, "chiefly of eastern New York, which she knew best." She helped Frank take observations for Mr. Willard, who was official observer for the National Weather Bureau. She lent a hand in the clubs, and received many a confidence which she vowed to keep eternally secret. It was to her Frank confided at fourteen the conviction that she (Frank) had been "born to a fate."

One week end Mr. Willard, who was still in the legislature, brought home a card announcing the opening of a private school for boys. The card was bordered with a Latin sentence, which he translated: "Knowledge is power, and labor conquers all things." Frank repeated the Latin till she could say it to her father's satisfaction. She pondered it. The way out of this wilderness, then, this isolation, was through knowledge? She would get knowledge.

When Miss Burdick left them at the end of two years, the Willards felt that the next step was to dignify education in the eyes of their children. With Mr. Inman's help, Mr. Willard built a little brown schoolhouse a mile away. "It was plain and inviting," says his daughter, "that little bit of a building standing under the trees on the river bank. Inside, pine desks were ranged along the wall — boys on one side, girls on the other, a slight platform with a rude desk taking up the end nearest the door. But this schoolhouse was a wonder in our eyes, a temple of learning, a telescope through which we were to take our first peep at the world outside of home."

On the opening day, to add to the thrill of "going away from home" to school, Oliver took the girls that mile in a bob-sleigh drawn by a yoke of oxen. On the steps of the school they saw nine other children. Soon they were joined by Professor Hodge, who carried a dinner pail and an armful of books. His piercing eyes, his pleasant smile and melodious voice won them. His long blue coat with its brass buttons quite set him off from anyone else Frank had seen. It seemed to emphasize the fact that he was "a real Yale graduate," qualified to give them the advantages other folks enjoyed. As he stood on the steps ringing the bell "long, loud, and merrily," her heart bounded with happiness. A man who had taught at Oberlin was going to teach *them!* He gave them four months of inspiration. He was followed by his sister-in-law, Miss Hovey.

Presently came a winter in a "select school" in Janesville. Then a summer in the home of the Whitmans, teachers from Georgia who were vacationing six miles from Forest Home. Here Frank began the study of French and made the acquaintance of what was to her a new form of literature, the novel. Promptly she was to feel her father's disapproval when he found her reading *Villette*. Taking the book from her, he addressed himself to the astonished Mrs. Whitman: "Never let my daughter see that book again, if you please, madam." But the seed had been planted. It would sprout.

The climax to this unique educational progression was music lessons at the state Institute for the Blind, a mile away, the only place within reach for such instruction. The teacher, Frank Campbell, was a brilliant blind pianist who gave concerts; he even had engagements abroad. Frank liked him. But it was with a wrench of her heartstrings that she watched the dear old melodeon give place to an "elegant" new piano, bought with the advice of Mr. Whitman.

Mrs. Willard was not given to preachments, but once she said to the children: "I, too, had ambitions, but I have *buried* myself on this farm — disappearing from the world, to reappear in my children, I trust."

"You shall, mother!" they assured her glibly.

"But that means hard work on your part," she warned. "It means *investing* your time instead of *spending* it."

The wisdom of her idea was to grow with the years — investing time, not spending it.

On Frank's sixteenth birthday she confided to her journal (consoler of broken hearts): "This is my birthday and the date of my martyrdom. Mother insists that at last I must have my hair 'done up woman-fashion.' She says she can hardly forgive herself for letting me 'run wild' so long. We had a great time over it, and here I sit, like another Samson, 'shorn of my strength.' That figure won't do, for the greatest trouble with me is that I shall never be shorn again. My back hair is twisted up like a corkscrew; I carry eighteen hairpins; my head aches miserably; my feet are entangled in the skirt of my hateful new gown. I am never to jump over a fence again as long as I live.

As for chasing the sheep down in the shady pasture, it's out of the question, and to climb to my 'Eagle's Nest' in the big burr oak would ruin this new frock beyond repair. Altogether, I recognize that my 'occupation's gone.' "

It was, therefore, a budding young lady, a rural debutante, who welcomed the relatives from the East, Josiah's brother Zophar and his wife and two sisters who came to see "how Josiah's folks were getting along." With what grand discussions the brothers enlivened the evenings — Zophar the Whig and Josiah the Democrat; Zophar the Congregationalist and Josiah the Methodist, differences of grave moment in those days. For hours at a time they recalled incidents of their boyhood, hours of never ending entertainment for the girls (Oliver was now a student at Beloit College), when they learned much about their ancestors and the part those venerable people had played in the making of New England.

There was Major Simon Willard, for one, who had come to America in 1634 and settled at Concord, Massachusetts, where he held many positions of trust. His motto was, "Truth for authority, not authority for truth." There were Solomon Willard, the architect of Bunker Hill Monument, and Elijah Willard, chaplain in the Revolution and pastor of a church at Dublin, New Hampshire, for forty years. Fine minds and inflexible wills had characterized all the Willard line, men true to their name, "one who wills."

Yet none of the Willards had been more courageous, Mrs. Willard reminded them gently, than her grandfather, Nathaniel Thompson, who was but a lad at the outbreak of the Revolution. Once at a dinner where the king's health had been proposed and glass had clinked glass as the toast went round, young Nathaniel rose and cried, "To George Washington's health, and *it* shall go round!" Instead of clinking their glasses, they drove him from the room, and would have done him injury had he not escaped them.

There was the Willard motto: "*Gaudet patientia duris,*" which Josiah translated for the girls: "Patience rejoices in hardships." Here was a new idea for Frank to store away with that earlier Latin saying, "Knowledge is power." She had not yet learned patience of that kind.

Zophar's visit ended all too soon, and with the departing guests went Mrs. Willard also. It seemed inconceivable that the home could exist without her; it never had. But she had been "buried" on that farm ten long years. Her husband thought it time she was resurrected.

To strangers Mr. Willard seemed a grave, rather stern man; never to his children. During his wife's absence, he gave himself up to the girls. He made javelins and taught the girls to throw them; with great labor he constructed a mechanical toy to illustrate perpetual motion. When the girls went to tend the sheep, he went with them; if they carried lunch to the men in the fields, he helped them. If business took him to Janesville, the girls dressed up and went along. For their sake, perhaps, he stopped to call on friends in town.

But when shortly his wife was in the East again Mr. Willard surprised his daughters one day by saying, "I am going East to see the folks. You may as well come along." The girls had never been on a train, save to the state fair at Madison. Great was their excitement when a new trunk arrived for them. Into it went several things more important than clothes, among them Mary's drawing board and paints and Frank's manuscripts — poems, and a novel of the Wild West patterned on some books of Oliver's.

The fortnight Mr. Willard could be away was crowded with new experiences for the girls. Often after their return they amused themselves with comparisons between the East, governed by tradition, and the West — " of no history," as their cousins said.

That trip had done for them something they could not yet realize, though their parents did. Treading the same paths, roaming the same fields, sleeping in the same beds as their ancestors — " the saints and patriots and wits of old " — had made an indelible impress on their susceptible minds. Frank felt that she had thought the thoughts of her forebears, had felt their longings, had cherished their ideals. She had found something to which to anchor her " adventurous bark."

About the time of Frank's farewell to girlhood, she and Mary stood at the window one morning to see Oliver off to cast his first ballot — for John C. Fremont, Free-Soiler. Dressed in his best, Oliver sat beside his father, while behind them rode the farm hands, also on their way to vote. Mrs. Willard stayed at home. As Frank thought of the significance of the day she felt a lump in her throat, and could not see the wagon for the blur before her eyes.

Turning to Mary she asked, " Wouldn't you like to vote, as well as Oliver? Don't you and I love the country as well as he? And doesn't the country need our votes? "

This was not the first time Frank's proud spirit had felt the humiliation of being a " female." Three years before she had watched with a heavy heart Oliver's preparations for college — the arrival of the new suit from a Janesville tailor; the packing of the new trunk, to which each of the family had contributed something; the loading of the wagon with the furniture for his room, including a wood stove. From the porch she had watched her father and her brother clamber to the seat and wave good-by. In her grief there was a bitter tang.

"It would have been better," she said to her mother, "if Oliver and I had gone together."

They had read the same books at home; why not at college? She was just as quick to learn as he, just as good at remembering, just as keen at reasoning — unless in mathematics, which she hated. Why shouldn't they have the same opportunity to "invest their time"? Guessing her thoughts, Mrs. Willard answered, "You, too, must go away to school, my child. I wish it might be to Oberlin." But that, Frank knew, would involve too much expense. Where then? They waited two years for the answer.

Meanwhile, Frank consoled herself with the books Oliver brought home from Beloit at each vacation. She had read all Shakespeare's plays (some twice) and all the books of travel and biography in her father's bookcase. Oliver's library was far more varied. It brought to her and Mary poetry, history, essays, and Bohn's translations of the classics, besides an encyclopedia to browse in. Best of all, through Lord Chesterfield's *Letters on Politeness,* it brought intimate knowledge of a world they longed to enter. This book they read and reread.

They missed Oliver, especially in the evening. He had joined in their games or read aloud. He was given to bright sayings, too, that called forth laughter. He, best of them all, could take Frank down a peg when she needed it. Industrious yet easygoing, he would have been quite content to become a good farmer, but his parents would not hear of it. College, and then, perhaps, the ministry, which had been denied his father.

Frank found further consolation in writing what Oliver teasingly called "pomes." On the threshold of her eighteenth birthday she wrote one in free verse that portrays her restless spirit, champing at the bit:

I AM EIGHTEEN

"The last year is passed;
The last month, week, day, hour, and moment.
For eighteen years, quelling all thoughts
And wishes of my own,
I've been obedient to the powers that were.
Not that the yoke was heavy to be borne
And grievous,
Do I glory that 'tis removed —
For lighter ne'er did parents fond
Impose on child.
It was a *silver* chain;
But the bright adjective
Takes not away the *clanking* sound
That follows it.
There is a God — an uncreated life
That dwells in mystery.
Him, as a part of His vast, boundless Self,
I worship, scorning not, nor yet reluctantly
Paying my vows to the Most High.
And this command by Him imposed,
'Children, obey your parents,'
I receive and honor. . . .

But now, having through waitings long
And hopings manifold
Arrived here at the limit of minority,
I bid it now and evermore adieu,
And, sinful though it may be,
Weep not nor sigh
As it fades with the night. . . .

The clock has struck!
O heaven and earth, I'm free!
And here beneath the watching stars I feel
New inspiration. Breathing from afar
And resting on my spirit as it ne'er
Could rest before, comes joy profound.
And now I feel that I'm alone, and free
To worship and obey Jehovah only. . . ."

This new independence she put to the test at once.

"Toward evening on this 'freedom day,'" she says, "I took my seat quietly in mother's rocking chair, and began to read Scott's *Ivanhoe*. Father was opposed to story-books, and on coming in, he scanned this, while his brow grew cloudy.

"'I thought I told you not to read novels, Frances,' he remarked seriously.

"'So you did, father, and in the main I've kept faith with you in this. But you forget what day it is.'

"'What day, indeed! I should like to know if the day has anything to do with the deed?'

"'Indeed it has — I am eighteen — I am of age — I am now to do what I think is right. And to read this fine historical story is, in my opinion, a right thing for me to do.'

"My father could hardly believe his ears. At first he was inclined to take the book away, but that would do harm he thought instead of good. So he concluded to see this *novel* action from the funny side, and laughed heartily, Oliver doing the same, and both saying in one breath, 'A chip of the old block!'"

Thenceforth, Frances was to be "master of her fate."

(III)

College at Last

Now the tempo of Frank's life changes, as she emerges from isolation into the world. Each year has more to record of aspiration and achievement. The threads that ran hit-or-miss in childhood now begin to weave a pattern.

The final episode in the girls' home education began when Sarah Hill, the aunt they had left behind in Oberlin, came to Forest Home. History was her specialty, but she set Frank to work on several other subjects: mathematics, English derivatives, astronomy, physical geography, and a stiff course in what savored of theology, if Dick's *Future State* and *Christian Philosophy* are samples. They were certainly not much like *Villette.*

Then came the chance to go to college. Miss Hill was made professor of history in Milwaukee Female College and took the girls with her. Little is said of that first college, save that the Willard girls won instant popularity. Nor was this popularity due to any display of wealth, for the combined pin money of the two for the term was fifty cents, given them at parting by Mike, the hired man. "What do you need of money?" Mr. Willard had asked with amusement; "I pay the bills." But Frank found immediate use for her twenty-five cents. Fifteen went for candy and a ticket to the circus; the remaining ten was invested in a notebook for her essays. One of these was read at the close of the term. It bore the characteristic title, "Originality of Thought and Action."

Mr. and Mrs. Willard liked the college and its honor system

of government. Frank threw herself wholeheartedly into the study of botany, geology, and history, seeking always to excel. But when they went home for the Christmas holidays the girls heard they were not to return to Milwaukee. Sarah Hill was going back East.

The change of plan may have been due to Cousin Morilla Hill's visit. Cousin Morilla was most enthusiastic over a college at Evanston, Illinois — a college as yet but two years old, which offered a curriculum equivalent to those of Harvard and Yale. Equivalent, not identical. For the president believed that, though of equal ability with men, women had certain needs and aptitudes different from men's. This was an opinion in which Mr. Willard heartily concurred. To the Willards, as to most Americans in those days, Harvard and Yale (then only colleges) represented the acme and pitch of perfection in education. They could not know that Frank would live to see the high schools of the future outstrip in opportunities these early colleges, while colleges grew into universities.

To judge fairly a college of the fifties, one must remember that the natural sciences were in their infancy, social science was as yet unrecognized, music and art were "ornamental" branches, commercial studies were not thought of as college material. A college course consisted of Greek and Latin, higher mathematics, mental and moral philosophy, history, and elementary science usually without laboratory work.

After considering the curriculum, Mr. Willard weighed carefully the expense. Tuition, room and board for each student, $164 a year; modern languages, music and art extra; bookkeeping also extra, but recommended as an aid in keeping the accounts which each girl had to submit each week to her division teacher.

The more Cousin Morilla talked — and she was a good talker

— the stronger grew Mr. Willard's conviction that he must see this Northwestern Female College for himself, and talk with the young man at its head. Partly by wagon, partly by train, he reached the budding village of Evanston, with its plank sidewalks, its one country store, its little white-spired church, and its twenty or more families, all Methodists like himself. At the north end of the village was a divinity school; at the south end, Northwestern Female College; on the main street, Northwestern University. All were Methodist, but each was independent of the others. By far the handsomest of the three was the college. Indeed, it alone was handsome. Mr. Willard liked everything about it. Its architecture, pure colonial, reminded him of New England. Its grove of fifty oaks was distinctly midwestern. Beyond the driveway, the yellow dunes of Lake Michigan with their stunted cedars enhanced the roar and shimmer of the lake stretching to the horizon. Never again would he be satisfied till he came to dwell beside this inland sea — as near it as possible.

Twelve miles from Chicago, Evanston was at a safe distance from worldly temptations. It was further protected by the university's charter forbidding the sale of liquor within four miles of that institution. As for the college, its equipment was up to date, its scholastic and ethical standards were high, its teachers above the average. The "Squire" especially liked the president; he and "Professor" — as President Jones was always called — held like views on religion, politics and education.

Josiah Willard was not the man to overpraise his children. He did, however, tell "Professor" that Frances had won a prize from the Illinois Agricultural Society for the best essay on "The Embellishment of a Country Home." The girl had seen their own home grow, he explained, "from nothing to a bower of beauty." With the medal and cup had come a note congratulating " a lady so young on an achievement so creditable." This they valued more than the prize. The proud father may also have told of his daughter's declaration of independence on her eighteenth birthday, and his acknowledgment that she was a chip of the old block. At all events, liking " the old block," President Jones looked forward to seeing the " chips."

They came. On March 2, 1858, they "left Forest Home . . . ," says Miss Willard — " the old-fashioned homestead where I dreamed my dream of dreams." The reminiscence is tinged with sadness. But the day of leaving had no sadness, only the excitement of breakfasting at three in the morning, saying good-by to Bridget and the farm hands, breaking from mother's tight embrace to clamber into the farm wagon and wave handkerchiefs till home and folks melted into the haze of distance.

After the wagon ride to Janesville came the train ride to Chicago, an ugly, sprawling town of frame and brick, though to them a metropolis. Then dinner at the Matteson House, Chicago's best (though now ignored by historians), where the two country girls were so overawed by the white-clad waiters that Mr. Willard had to order for them.

A few hours later found them getting settled in their college room. They had not, like Oliver, brought their own furniture. The college, in line with the best institutions of the East, had furnished such unusual conveniences as a clothes closet and bookshelves in each room. Below the shelfful of poke bonnets the girls hung their voluminous dresses. They filled the bureau drawers with petticoats and red flannel underwear, leaving a corner for their long-fringed shawls. The hanging shelves received the few books they had brought. On their knees they tacked down the carpet for which they had helped sew the rags. It brought home nearer, that rag carpet. Each color suggested a garment some one of them had worn: a wrapper of their mother's, their father's old jeans, the suit Oliver discarded when he went to college. They fell silent as one stretched and the other tacked.

The day was cold; they must build a fire in the wood stove so like their stoves at home. From the end of the hall they brought wood and kindling. While Frank made the fire, Mary filled the pitcher from one of the pails near the freight elevator, and the lamp from the hall's kerosene can. Now for the bed. These sheets and pillowcases they had seen their mother make; she had filled these pillows with feathers from their own geese. Mary had helped piece the quilts; they had all tied the comforters. Overwhelmed by memories, Mary ducked her head into a pillow to hide her tears.

Mr. Willard took them to the Reynolds House for supper. Then they bade him good-by. At ten the retiring bell rang. All lights and fires out now. In the dark, red head and brown lay close together, the brown one shaken by sobs, but not the red.

Next morning at the ringing of the breakfast bell, each Willard prepared to descend to the dining-room with her silver fork (which the circular stipulated should be distinctly marked and cost not more than fifty cents), her napkin and her silver napkin-ring. Mary, calm and smiling, seems not to have been at all embarrassed on entering the room where fifty girls and ten teachers stood behind their chairs awaiting the signal to be seated. Frank, on the other hand, was painfully conscious of her red hair, her country manners and her country-made clothes. To hide her embarrassment she assumed a haughtiness that repelled all advances.

After breakfast came chapel. Here they heard the rules

read. " A good many," Mary confided to her journal, " but I guess we can keep them." Frank fastened a copy to their door for future reference. To girls who had lived without obvious restraint the very thought of rules was distasteful. Soon, however, that dislike was offset by their admiration for Professor and his wife, both still in their twenties. He was a scholar but not a pedant; like them, he had a keen sense of humor. Mrs. Jones, plump, rosy, and jolly, had a lively give-and-take of jokes and laughter. Yet these two young people, no older than some of their students, maintained an inborn dignity that set them apart.

Less than a month after her arrival Mary dared to " fool Professor " on April first. But she would never have dreamed of opposing his authority beyond the breaking of a petty rule or two, to which she smilingly confessed at chapel. When he died in his prime, Frank recalled him as " brotherly and kind, but always our President, inspiring to noble lives."

Hundreds of girls who came under his influence blessed him. Their affection through the years was to him a constant stimulus, his reward for the long struggle to create a larger opportunity for them. In 1855, while his father and brothers were erecting the building, he had canvassed the state to arouse an interest in sending girls to college. Often he had spoken to deaf ears; often he had been denied even an audience. But the dike of prejudice having once been pierced, there began a steady flow of students.

A generation later, Frances Willard wrote: " The higher education of women was a new idea in 1855. . . . How much it meant, then, that at the very beginning of the active educational movement here [at Evanston], even on October 29, 1855, the ' Northwestern Female College ' quietly took its place as one among a trio of schools, founded in the name of Christian education and having the whole Northwest as their territory of supply. . . . With no forceful businessmen back of the enterprise, no real-estate bonds, no distinguished names adorned with 'lunar fardels' to lend prestige [all of which its neighbor Northwestern University had] it moved all the same (not welcome overmuch) and came to stay. . . ."

President Jones was professor of Greek; Mrs. Jones, of Latin. But the Willard girls were taking neither, since to their mother "dead" languages were dead indeed. She had urged they take all they could of English literature. Frank, however, never ceased to regret the fun she had missed — the fun of making a dead language come alive. All her life she quoted Latin now and then, as if she liked the feel of it on her tongue. In deference to their mother's wishes, the girls took the scientific course, having already a sound foundation of natural science.

In *Glimpses of Fifty Years* Miss Willard "glimpses" their favorite teachers: Mary Dickinson, "of queenly grace and fine abilities"; Lydia Hayes, graduate teacher much beloved and Mrs. Jones' sister; intellectual Lizzie Mace McFarland, later acting president, admiration for whom "alone made mathematics endurable." Dearest of all was Luella Clark, well known as a poet among Methodists. Officially she was professor of literature and philosophy; unofficially she was adviser to all would-be writers and confidante of all who needed a friend older and wiser than themselves. These were the women under whose influence Frank was, in time, to develop the charm that would capture thousands. As yet she was only a crude country girl with much of the tomboy about her.

Regarding her childhood and budding womanhood, Frank and her mother are our sole authorities. In Evanston, however, Frank was soon recognized as a girl who was going to make her mark in the world. Thenceforth, many are the records of her doings and sayings.

Louisa Dake was first of the college girls to see the Willards. They and she boarded the same train for Evanston, where she, too, was entering the Northwestern Female College. Assigned rooms across the hall from each other, they were thrown much together. Louisa describes their first meal at college, as earlier comers looked them over, scanning critically their faces, their dress, their manners. Many of the girls were farmers' daughters, but not a few came from Kenosha, Joliet and Waukegan, centers of wealth and refinement.

The Willard " personality-plus " attracted much attention. What Louisa thought she wisely kept to herself, till Frank asked her bluntly. Pressed to tell the truth, Louisa told it — tactlessly, she admits, since she need not have said Frank was homely, a fact the sensitive girl knew too well already. Frank " rose with a flushed face and walked away." For some days the two did not speak as they passed each other. But eventually they became warm friends. From her association with this well informed girl who was always wanting to peer below the surface of things, Louisa says, she herself took to questioning the sands on the beach, the stones they skipped on the lake, the stars they gazed at from the cupola. Gentle, lighthearted Mary was always with her dashing sister.

A still dearer friend than Louisa was Mary Bannister, who was later to marry the marvelous Oliver. It is she who tells of Frank's assumption of haughtiness to conceal her embarrassment, though in class Frank dropped the mask, her face lighted with enthusiasm, words flowed freely. If sometimes Frank overheard others praise her scholarship, it served to soothe her proud spirit and set it free to seek friends, despite the looks and clothes she deemed such a handicap.

Mr. Willard still held the exasperating idea that he was qualified to shop for his daughters. On the farm this had mattered little; life had been so full of things more important than clothes. But now, among fifty or more critics — none too lenient — of dress and manners, as well as of brains, Frank was humiliated by his bad taste. To Mary it did not matter; she was pretty and could wear anything.

One day their father sent the girls two red hoods, just alike. Mary looked fairly well in hers; but on Frank the hood was a "scream." She stood the laughter at her expense, till one girl went too far. Frank knocked her down, and defiantly tied the obnoxious hood the tighter on her red hair. Soon after, she followed the new fashion and had her hair bobbed. Mr. Willard's only comment when he heard of it was, "The fool and her hair are soon parted."

Years after, Frances confessed in *How to Win*: "The plain-faced girl who has a pretty sister commands my inmost sympathy; for just there I have been, and in a soul most sensitive and timid have hidden away the pathos. . . . To have beside you, nearer than any other human being, a sister, fair and winsome, whose ribbons always 'match,' whose hair takes kindly to the latest style, whose gloves invariably fit, and whose bonnet cannot be unbecoming; to know yourself for a creature awkward and unadorned, upon whom this gracious, loving comrade at your side vainly expends all the skill of fingers, deft and delicate — this is not what a girl's heart would choose. To hear the door-bell ring at evening, and see from upper windows the freshly garnished young collegian enter, asking for 'Miss Mary'; to be counted out so often when she is counted in, . . . this is to give to a girl's heart 'thoughts that do often lie too deep for tears.'"

Within a month of her arrival Frank was editor of the

college paper and leader of those who considered themselves the "intellectuals." "Fascinating!" said the girls. "Brilliant!" said her teachers. And what of Frank and the head of the institution? Each took the other's measure. Each paid the other the tribute of admiration — she, self-willed and accustomed to lead; he, self-disciplined and authorized to lead. Professor recognized how tactful and patient those must be who would train this spirited colt of a girl. Whether he wished it or not, *she* would lead the girls. He must direct, not challenge, that leadership. Mary Bannister testifies that he came, in time, to rely on Frank's influence and good sense to counteract the tendency to silly escapades, such as moonlight walks with university boys; and that, in time, Frank, because of a "dashing recklessness" that gave her fascination, became as popular as a university senior. By then, she was as carefully dressed and neatly gloved as any of them.

Before that, however, there was a period of maladjustment when — in Methodist parlance — she "fell from grace." For a term she was under the spell of a girl named Maggie, who dared her to be a law unto herself. Rules, argued Maggie, were a device to keep order among the mediocre. If *they* maintained order without rules there was no cause for complaint. Soon Frank found herself leader of a group of girls who eschewed rules. At chapel, when those who had broken rules were expected to rise and confess, the "wild" girls, as the "good" girls called them, remained seated.

It was during this wayward period that once, during study hours, Frank dressed herself and Maggie as pirates. From her trunk — a strange comment on how little she had changed as yet — she drew high-top boots, red sashes, wooden bowie knives and pistols. On the table between them she set a bottle of ginger ale, substitute for whisky. Knees crossed, they smoked long cigars and talked in language borrowed from yellow-backed *Jack Shepard.*

A knock at the door and, without waiting for an answer, Miss Dickinson entered, Frank's division teacher. What a spectacle! Frank Willard, star student, outlandishly dressed and hobnobbing with the wildest girl in school! Miss Dickinson, however, had tact, and Frank, looking at this teacher she loved, thought again how " queenly " she was.

" This is fortunate! " Miss Dickinson cried, apparently delighted. " The mosquitoes have almost driven me out of my room this hot night. If you girls will come and smoke them out, it will be a great favor to me."

So the " pirates," cigars in hand, clumped down the hall after this exquisite woman. Sitting uneasily in her room they smoked, and smoked, and smoked, while their teacher, towel in hand, shooed the mosquitoes real and imaginary through the open window. There the incident ended. It was never alluded to. Soon after Maggie was dropped.

At the end of the term Professor called for term reports on deportment. Mary, " merry saint of the school," was one of those who rose and pleaded guilty. The " wild " girls sat still. But Professor knew, and Frank knew he knew.

She was reading Emerson's *Essays* just then. Perhaps one day she happened upon the sentence, " To live as one likes is plebeian; the noble man aspires to law and order." If there was one thing she dreaded, it was to seem plebeian; at heart she coveted nobility. Her study of science, too, enforced the nobility of obedience to law.

Four months of rather tame lawlessness was enough. Professor had guessed rightly that such would be her reaction. She was too intelligent to be satisfied with anything but the best.

(IV)

Undergraduate Days

THE THREE QUALITIES IN FRANCES WILLARD THAT IMPRESSED Gamaliel Bradford most when he was preparing to enshrine her among his famous American women were her charm, her simplicity and her joy in achievement. Childhood and college activities demonstrated her ability to do, and to enjoy what she had done. Her simplicity appeared as frankness, directness, and freedom from affectation. But the charm so manifest in her maturity was not evident in college days. She delighted both old and young with her dash and sparkle; they were proud to be numbered among her friends. That elusive something called charm, however, so rare, so exquisite, was yet to be born — out of loss and suffering and sacrifice.

She preferred books to people. People annoyed her with their trivialities; in books " the best self of the author meets the best self of the reader." At Forest Home she had read great writers of all ages. But in those first months at college she met a new writer who " enchanted " her. Margaret Fuller Ossoli's *Memoirs* revealed the kind of person she, Frances Willard, wanted to be.

" Oh, to have known such a woman! " she wrote in her journal, ". . . to possess such a mind! Here we see what a woman achieved for herself. Not so much fame or honor — these are of minor importance — but a whole character: a cultivated intellect, right judgment, self-knowledge, self-happiness. If she, why not we, by steady toil? "

Against her will, she was impressed with the significance of the saying, "No man liveth to himself." The social life of the college, the social life of the village, demanded her participation. She argued the case in her journal: There were two worlds, in each of which she must take a part — the world of scholarship, where "men ponder, delve, and discover" in secret, the world where she felt at home; and the world called "society," where men gather for amusement and relaxation, the world where one must have accomplishments — a story, a joke, a song, conversation — the world from which she shrank. "Society is not for scholarly discipline. Society is to everyday life what recess is to the schoolboy" — not incidental, not unimportant, but "the outward sign of an inward grace" that finds its expression in good-fellowship.

She threw herself into the social life of the college: the Sunday evening open house, the parties, the literary society. She had a good voice; she was a fair pianist; she talked well on topics that interested her; she could joke; she was an intelligent listener.

One college function was the "Grammar Party," a device to popularize better speech. The diction of young people from farms and villages of the then Northwest was not above reproach, and the college waged constant warfare to preserve the purity of the King's — or rather the Queen's — English. Anyone who murdered it was fined a penny — five cents, if a teacher. If wrongly accused, she collected double from her accuser. This money went to pay for the "Cake of Errors" which was the chief ornament of the refreshment table and was carved with great ceremony.

At one of these parties Frank and Mary helped serve; then each held a candle for the readers of the special edition of the college paper. Mary's journal enlarged upon the festoons of evergreen she had helped make, the food, the festivities which had lasted till midnight. Frank's account, on the other hand, was a dismal tale of a tight dress nearly ruined in serving, rooms so hot she almost fainted, relief that the hundred and fifty guests had departed at last. She ended, "To books let me flee. They never frighten."

Sunday had its full religious program, beginning with church. Fifty girls in hoopskirts, poke bonnets and heavily fringed shawls marched in procession two by two with their professors, to the little white-spired church three blocks away. The woodland had been cut into squares by dirt streets and board sidewalks, but there were few houses along the route. At the church the procession halted, then passed in single file up the narrow aisle to seats reserved for the college. At two o'clock came Bible class, after which those who could were asked to read their Greek Testaments for an hour. Frank envied them.

Mindful of the many lonely young men at the university and the Biblical Institute, the Joneses kept open house Sunday evenings. Gentlemen properly introduced might call on the young ladies Saturday afternoon or evening; Sunday they were the guests of the college. In this, as in all other gatherings, Mary joined with alacrity, Frank with reluctance.

In the Minerva Literary Society, however, Frank was in her element. Whether there fell to her lot essay, declamation, poem or debate, she worked on it with zest. She shone in the debates held in the church, filled to overflowing at such times. She and Julia Atkins were acclaimed the school's best debaters.

As the end of the year drew near, President Jones, having as yet but one graduate, chose the Willard girls to take part in the Commencement program — Frank for her originality, Mary for her winsomeness. To the girls this meant not only the preparation of essays, but the need for new dresses as well — white dresses with sashes. Frank wrote her father to that effect. His reply threw the girls and their friends into a gale of laughter:

"Frances, your letter of eighteen dollars notoriety nearly upset my equanimity, and I was on the point of sending for you to come home, but upon second thought concluded to forward six dollars to Miss Dickinson to buy the material for your dresses — which will be amply sufficient, and more too. As for the sashes, I shall buy them, if necessary. I am somewhat at a loss whether or not to ask Professor Jones whether he prefers to have your tuition and board bills paid, or to have twenty or thirty dollars paid to fix you up in white for the Commencement! I am quite sure what his choice would be. The fact is I have no money. I have sold some wheat for fifty cents per bushel to get money for actual necessaries. 'You can't have more of a cat than her skin.' Candy! Candy! Candy! Mary looks serious. What shall I say? Wheat at fifty cents per bushel to buy candy for farmers' daughters!!!

"Eighteen dollars! My horrors! That is a pretty serious prelude to the perpetuation of college honors. I am done and say no more. . . . All in tolerable health. Bridget 'sings praises' and Mike says 'Oh!' and John looks amazed as they hear of all your goings on. Your Affectionate Father"

It must have been a pretty sight when on Commencement day the college family moved in procession through the woodsy village to the church. First, the president and the board of trustees in black Prince Alberts and stovepipe hats. Next, the faculty, their figured silks contrasting with the equally wide-hooped white dresses of the essayists and singers behind them. Last of all, the undergraduates, in flowered muslins, black slippers and lace mitts.

Bordering the sidewalks were onlookers from the surrounding country. In carriages and farm wagons they had driven in from Chicago and Waukegan, from Libertyville and other towns older than Evanston. They had come early and left their baskets of picnic lunch in the woods adjoining the college, where tables had been built for them. Mr. and Mrs. Willard were there, as they were always at the Beloit Commencement.

Into the church and up the aisles moved the procession — undergraduates to the college seats, the others to the great platform built out over the front seats. No speaker had been engaged for the occasion; president and students furnished the program. As each girl finished, friends threw bouquets upon the platform, nosegays from their own gardens. Then President Jones delivered his baccalaureate address and farewell to the one graduate. The benediction was pronounced. The school year was over, save for the president's levee that evening.

A year hence Frank would graduate; two years hence it would be Mary's turn. And then? They little dreamed what.

That summer Louisa Dake spent two weeks at Forest Home. Frank was teaching in the little brown schoolhouse, and " Louie " was left much to herself in the low, rambling house and among the pets. It was still the custom in that part of the country for the one desiring to teach to solicit pupils at so much a head, this being the teacher's sole remuneration. So Frank had put on her sunbonnet and gone from farm to farm till she had promise of at least twelve children. Twelve children at a dollar each would furnish her pin money for a year.

Louisa draws an amusing picture of the teacher tilted back in her chair, several saplings lying on her desk, evidently for dramatic effect only, as the children were " good little things " who " ducked their heads and giggled " at their teacher's funny sayings. Once, after Miss Willard had become nationally known, she sent out a seasonal card decorated with the four-part round " Scotland's Burning," as a memento of her first teaching experience. Louisa, seeing it, was reminded of how the woods had rung with the cry, " Fire! Fire! Fire! Fire! " while hands and heads had bobbed now to right and now to left.

But there was a sadness about that summer, too. The Willards were leaving Forest Home forever. For a year Mrs. Willard had been maneuvering to bring her brood together again. It was time she was resurrected from the farm where she had been buried. She and " Mr. Willard " must live in Evanston. Oliver, too, was shortly to come there to begin his studies at Garrett Biblical Institute. So Mr. Willard built a home on the lake shore, rather better than most in Evanston, a real " residence." He was now a broker associated with a leading bank in Chicago. Building on ground once swamp, he called the home " Swampscott." With tireless pains he laid out the grounds, as he had those at Forest Home. The broad lawn demanded pails on pails of water. The trees, aside from native oaks, he brought from the farm, and planted with Frank's help. What had been a marsh became an estate.

In the large front bedroom overlooking the lake the girls set up their household gods. At opposite corners were their desks, Mary's a homemade affair of pine boards, Frank's the handsome secretary that had graced her father's sanctum at Forest Home. Seated at it, she drew in her journal a picture of the room: piles of books; pictures and daguerreotypes; Mary's sketchboard; Oliver's hunting knife and college cane, both discarded now; the canary splitting their ears with his song.

The girls were now emancipated from the most irksome of the college rules. Yet — such is human nature — Frank liked to recall " the joyful old times " when she had been a " boarder." Shortly the name of J. F. Willard appeared in the college catalogue as trustee, soon after as treasurer of the board, and so remained till his death.

The December number of the *Casket and Budget,* the college

paper, was *printed,* and the students solicited subscriptions from home. But the country was suffering another depression, and such a luxury as a rather crude college paper found no market at a dollar and a half a year, much as parents enjoy seeing their daughters in print. Nevertheless, this issue of the *Casket and Budget* is recognized as the " first paper printed in Evanston." Subsequent issues returned to manuscript form. One printed copy and one in script survive, the latter tied with wide flowered, picot-edged ribbon.

The editors felt quite proud of that printed issue, which had run advertisements enough to pay for the printing. " Our Friend Thomas " advertised his goods in couplet rhyme. Since he sold everything from fish-hooks to furniture, it had been easy enough to find rhymes for twenty-two items: nails — pails; balls — awls; chains — reins; mop-sticks — tooth-picks; " mice "-traps — percussion-caps. The final couplet sounds suspiciously Willardish:

> " And those who cannot ever pay
> Please take the hint and stay away."

News items, local hits, and even a bit of telegraphic news from New York offset the very sentimental essays and poems. The supreme hit was a parody on the Rules, signed " W " and written in the biblical form then popular for parody:

" Behold it came to pass in the first month of the fourth year of King William's reign . . . the King gathered them together . . . and did proclaim . . . ' O wicked and perverse generation. . . . Give ear and hear my words.' " Twenty-one rules follow, of which the most grievous and oftenest broken was, " Ye shall bridle your tongues seven and a half hours in each day and two in each night season."

When the paper was read, as usual from the platform, it is

said none laughed more heartily than "King William." Here was no censorship of the press.

It was the day of the autograph fad. The Iota Omega sorority, founded by Frank in imitation of Oliver's fraternity, met regularly at Mary Bannister's. Collecting autographs of celebrities was one of its nonsecret activities. Indeed, the replies it received were too good to hide. Horace Greeley sent a sharp reprimand, "which fortunately we could not entirely decipher," says Frank. From Abraham Lincoln, now nationally known through the Lincoln-Douglas debates, came a friendly letter; from Longfellow a stanza of "Excelsior" with his signature. Queen Victoria vouchsafed no reply.

A garden club, with a flower bed for each member, grew out of Frank's love of outdoors. A sheet of "Queries and Answers" aroused great enthusiasm. Frank thought up the queries; the others found the answers.

Here, as at Forest Home, Frances Willard's flair for organization, like the stones she loved to skip, made ever widening circles.

Frank's senior year was one of great strain. She was carrying extra work in order to graduate before she was twenty. Often she fell asleep on the floor, her head in a book — too often the argumentative Butler's *Analogy*. Early in the spring she wrote: "*I am and am to be* in a perpetual furor . . . no time to think steadily or do anything carefully and well. . . . I am tired and fretted, and I long for the rest that is to follow."

The result was a nervous breakdown followed by typhoid fever. It was her first severe illness. In consequence, she suffered two keen disappointments. The first was missing the wedding of Lydia Hayes, Mrs. Jones' sister. Frank was to have led the long line of bridesmaids. Bitterness was added by the fact that "Lillie" was marrying a missionary to India and Frank would see her no more for years.

A still harder blow was missing her own Commencement. How she had looked forward to appearing again on the stage garlanded with evergreen! She had not forgotten her "inward tumult of delight" a year ago, as bouquets from all parts of the church fell at her feet. Then she had been only supplemental, with Lillie Hayes the center of interest as first graduate of their college. What ecstasy she might have felt this year as valedictorian in her own class of two! The blow was too crushing.

The fact remained she *was* a graduate. "How very little does the word mean, and yet how much," she wrote. "It means years of patient, silent brain work, discipline, obedience to the will of others. It means that we have started on the beautiful search after truth and right and peace. Only started — only opened the door. . . . I shall be twenty in September, and I have as yet been of no use in the world. When I recover, I will earn my own living, 'pay my own way,' and try to be of use."

The determination to be of use was not new. When President Foster of the university had closed a sermon with the warning, "Brethren, with most men life is a failure," Frank had prayed that her life might not be such, that someone might have cause to thank God she had lived.

Freedom from restraint, which Frank had hailed, did not prove so satisfying as she had anticipated. To be sure, she could do as she pleased, but what did she please to do? She wrote: "Friends wait and watch, materfamilias fears, paterfamilias hopes. It is a time full of unuttered pathos." Later grew upon her the conviction that every girl, as well as every boy, should be trained for a vocation, as part of a liberal education. At twenty, however, she found few vocations open to women save teaching. Teaching she dreaded.

To be of use — the desire became an obsession. What was

she doing, she asked her journal. Who was wiser, better, happier because she lived? Yet what could she do? They kept a maid for housework; there were no young children to care for; Evanston had no poor. "Nobody needs me!" She must wait. . . . Her mood changes; she must not take herself too seriously; she laughs at her caged ambitions: "Thus having moralized, I lean back in my easychair and resume the reading of Poe's ghostly tales."

Weeks pass. She grows more and more restless. Once she had felt she was born to a fate. Now, college days over, she should be taking part in the world's work. Not for her the "happy mediocrity" their minister deplored. In honesty, as before God, she weighs herself:

"Jump into the scales, F. E. W., and you shall be weighed. *What you believe of yourself is vital to yourself*. . . . If you 'feel the victory in you,' as my father says, all things are possible. Then deal generously with yourself. Let not modesty (of which I think you have never been accused) cause you to pass lightly over any redeeming traits you may possess."

The self-analysis is long, but she tries to be honest. She knows she is not beautiful, not even good-looking — Mary to the contrary; but she has no unpleasant defects in face or figure (her red hair is turning to auburn on the way to the soft brown of maturity). She is reserved toward those to whom she is indifferent, but careful not to wound feelings — deferential to superiors, kind to inferiors, cordial with equals. In "society" she is stiff and unnatural.

"You have a good mind," she continues, "but not evenly balanced or developed. Your perceptions are rather quick, memory unusual, imagination good, reasoning faculties fair, judgment in practical matters not extraordinary, but elsewhere excellent. . . . As for your will . . . I hardly think it is particularly powerful . . . there is a sort of independence and self-reliance that gives the idea of will, and yet is really not such." Her devotion to her friends is warmer than they guess; she lacks an all-embracing love for man as man. She thinks herself " spasmodically generous but fundamentally selfish."

As for religion, she is inclined to skepticism and haunted by unbelief. It is the aesthetics of Christianity that attracts her, yet she longs to live a holy life. She ends with the injunction to herself to be gentle, kind, forgiving, and patient, hard as patience is for hasty tempers like hers and her father's.

In her journal for February, 1860, occurs the first mention of temperance since the childish pledge and the exclusion of saloons from Fort City. She was nearly twenty when she attended " almost the only " temperance lecture she had ever heard. Parker Earle, Chicago agent of the Illinois Temperance League, spoke in Evanston on the relation of government to society and temperance. Frank was pleased that he avoided all sentimental appeal and addressed himself to the intelligence of his audience. The statistics he quoted on Chicago's rum traffic were amazing to her. She awoke to a realization of how ignorant she was of the world around her.

A letter from Lillie Hayes Waugh pictured the condition of woman in India, and led Frank to reasoning how the status of woman determines civilization. Rebecca Harding Davis' *Life in the Iron Mills* had already revealed the life of the common people. And again she yearns: " Oh, that I were a Don Quixote in a better cause than his, or even a Sancho Panza to some mightier spirit who I trust will come upon the earth some day! "

Professor knew how sincerely Frank was seeking an anchor for her soul. When a shocked student had confided to him that Frank didn't know whether there was a God or whether the Bible was true, he had answered reassuringly, " If she will keep on trying to find out, she will find out." She was, he knew, at an age when every old belief must give a reason for its continuance or step aside. She would never be brought into the faith by "entreaties and importunities."

Winter had come again — the winter after Frank's graduation. It was Sunday evening. A large congregation had listened to an ordinary sermon, says Professor, and seemed impatient for dismissal, when in response to an invitation to unite with the church on probation, a young woman moved up the aisle to the altar. "There was no mistaking that form and face. It was Miss Willard. . . . The effect on the congregation was electrical . . . faces filled with joy; many an eye was moist. Someone began the Doxology — 'Praise God from whom all blessings flow' — and it was sung as if the very stars were expected to join the chorus."

After the nine months of probation exacted by her church, she — and Mary — were baptized and partook of their first communion. "Those were solemn vows we took," she wrote. "I felt how awful the responsibility that would henceforth rest upon us. And yet the ceremony seemed very beautiful to me. We knelt there at the altar, we whose lives and hearts and thoughts had been one. It was fitting that we should in this, as in everything, be together."

Evanstonians long remembered that scene — the pretty face crowned with soft brown hair, the plain face topped with red. All too soon Mary would be but a memory — Mary with her open, serene face, her studiousness, her little arts for making others happy, her wonder that people didn't do more to "make the world good." All too soon she and Frank would no longer do things together. But Mary's question would become a command: "Do something to make the world good." That command would largely determine the course of Frank's life.

(V)

The Girl Becomes a Woman

For the next fourteen years Frances Willard was a teacher. It was teach or do nothing, be nothing. She chose to be something. She argued the case thus: If she went away, suffered, was lonesome, tired, had responsibility she alone could bear, she might grow to be strong and earnest in practice, as she had been thus far in theory. " So here goes for a fine character! " she exulted.

Thirty years later she summarizes that period: " Between 1858, when I began, and 1874, when I forever ceased to be a pedagogue, I had thirteen separate seasons of teaching in eleven separate institutions and six separate towns, my pupils in all numbering about two thousand." She lists the positions. To forestall any misapprehension, she adds: " Nor did I ever relinquish any of these situations save of my own free will, and in every case but one, I had from the authorities a warm invitation to return. . . . A desire to learn the methods of different institutions and to see more of the world were the chief motives that led me into an experience so varied. It is also but fair to confess that routine has always been immensely irksome to me, and to be ' tied to a bell-rope ' an asphyxiating process, from which I vainly sought to escape, changing the spot only to keep the pain."

While Professor and his friend the county superintendent of schools were in search of a position for her, Frank carefully charted her course, drawing up rules for conducting a country school. Among them were:

"Never let your pupils feel that they understand you or know what to expect from you. Be a mystery to them. Invent punishments; resort to expedients they least expect.

"Demand explicit obedience . . . and never yield a point.

"Introduce general exercises. . . . When they all think alike by your command, you can do with them what you will.

"Give them a good deal of outside information on all sorts of topics, to liven them up all you can.

"Introduce gymnastic exercises . . . ever so much singing . . . rounds . . . sing the multiplication tables . . . the capitals . . . the boundaries. . . . Bring flowers and name the parts. . . . Teach them the bones of the human body, the rulers of all countries, and as many other things as I can think up."

Judging from her success, she was not such a dictator as the first rules suggest; it was her devices to "liven them up" that pupils and students remembered in afteryears.

The preparations for leaving home were exciting. She anticipated the adventure of facing hardships she had been spared thus far. She dreaded leaving mother, "who cares for me as no other human being ever did," and Mary, who also longed to be independent, to earn money of her very own. Mary, too, prayed to be guided to a larger life. And she was. But not the life she had had in mind.

When Frank set out for her first position at Harlem, Illinois, Mr. Willard (humiliated to have a daughter of his earning money when he could support her) accompanied her. "With his ideas of the protection that should be accorded women, he could not conceive of my going there alone, although I was in my twenty-first year" — and Harlem was only ten miles away. The school director met them at the station, and warned Frank that the boys were pretty rough and had driven away more than one teacher. This caused her some trepidation as she bade her father good-by and moved to her desk.

According to custom she opened school with a reading from the Bible, then, at random, chose the well known song "I Want to be an Angel," only to be inwardly convulsed by the incongruity of it in a school of "rough" boys. But perhaps her frail body aroused their chivalry. Perhaps her sense of humor won them, or those livening exercises. To her surprise — and that of the parents — there was small need of discipline. Only one boy required a whipping, and that she administered, though he was much larger and stronger than she.

If there were heartaches and loneliness — and there were — she hid them. She was getting the discipline she had craved, discipline with a vengeance when water leaked through the roof onto her desk, when there was no dry wood for the fire, when she walked home through mud over her shoe-tops. But when she and the daughter of the house where she boarded became friends, life grew brighter.

After two terms Oliver succeeded her at Harlem. "See that you do as well as Frances," her proud father said to him.

Frank is going farther from home — sixty miles away this time. Charles B. Woodruff, former head of the Wisconsin Institute for the Blind, where the girls of Forest Home studied music, is opening an academy at Kankakee, Illinois, and invites Frank to join his faculty. She likes the work, though it is heavy. Moreover, she has a thoroughly good time. She sings songs instead of psalms, talks "localisms" instead of morality and religion, plays chess instead of reading, laughs instead of thinking, spends more time doing up her hair than "exerting the right kind of influence." Two young men coming to enroll find her in jovial mood, and marvel when they learn she is a teacher, not a schoolgirl.

But she is hardly settled before she is called home by Mary's illness. So the lively Miss Willard leaves Kankakee Academy, not to return. The fact is physical discomforts are hard for her to endure. Battling wind and rain, tramping through mud, sitting in wet clothes are, Mrs. Willard thinks, not only hard but dangerous for her "slender" child. Yet in the spring Frank took the Harlem school again.

That was the spring marked by the fall of Fort Sumter. At the President's call for troops, Northwestern University students formed a company and marched away under the command of Alphonso Linn. Biblical students, Oliver among them, formed a company also, but for some reason were never called.

Mary's journal gives a vivid picture of the first war meeting. There were flag-raisings, the first being at the college. Trains ran on Sunday for the first time, to carry volunteers answering "Father Abraham's" call. But the Willard family was not much affected. Frank taught, Mary sketched, Oliver studied for the ministry, Mr. Willard commuted, and Mrs. Willard kept house, just as before Secession, save that prices were soaring.

Many have wondered whether Frances Willard was ever in love. She answers for herself. Before going to Harlem the first time, she lists among the experiences she has not yet had "a love affair, to sober me." A few months later in Kankakee she holds the conviction that "no woman ever knows the depths and richness of her nature until she has loved a man — better than her own life. Until she has done this, much of pain and want must be endured by her." She confesses: "I have never been in love; I have never shed a tear, or dreamed a dream, or

Frances and Mary Willard, about 1847

Frances Willard at 21

sighed, or had a sleepless hour for love. I never treasured any man in my heart until he became sacred to me, until his words were as oracles, his smiles as sunshine, his voice like music. . . . I was too cautious, loved my peace too well, remembered too frequently that I was made for something far more worthy than to spend a disconsolate life wasting my heart . . . upon a man who did not care for it. . . . I have known several men for whom I might have cared. . . . I have looked after them as they passed me on the street . . . in church . . . in society, and have thought, 'You might care for him, but remember, you must not.' . . . I have not known as yet what it is to lean on any being except God. In all my friendships I am the one relied on, the one who fights the battles, or would if there were any to fight. Yet every night I say to God in prayer, 'Sometime, if it pleases Thee, give me the love of a manly heart, of one I can trust. But, if this cannot be, make it up to me in some other way. Thou knowest what is right.' "

Once, after Maggie — her fellow "pirate" — had gone to New York, Frank confessed to her mother that she had written Maggie, "I love you more than life, better than God, more than I fear damnation." To which Mrs. Willard replied, "O Frank! Pray God you never love a man!"

Yet that was the very thing that happened to her the second time she was in Harlem. In June she returned home wearing a ring. By the following February, however, the ring was discarded. She had found that "intellectual comradeship was [not] sure to develop into unity of heart." Her lover, then studying for the ministry, was destined to climb to the highest office his church could bestow. But his spirit was not her spirit, his outlook on life was not hers. Sometime life was to force them to pull together in a great enterprise, but she would find the yoke intolerable and refuse longer to bend her neck to it.

So much for that love affair. After ending the brief account with a pun, she continues in her *Glimpses* in more serious mood: " Of the real romance of my life, unguessed save by a trio of close friends, these pages may not tell. When I have passed from sight, I would be glad to have it made known." It never was. Her papers were burned after her death, and carried the secret with them. Readers of her autobiography only know that in her late forties she met a man whose photograph always thereafter stood on her desk. But that is not conclusive evidence, is it?

She was evidently thinking of the man she loved when she said of her story of achievement, " I wanted someone else to know," and added, " I had to care about that other one, about his knowing too." Now that she had realized her desire to be " widely known, widely helpful and beloved," did she hope that he might rejoice in her success, though he might never guess her love? Nevertheless, when a sentimental woman said she wished she had a window in her heart, that all might see her love, Miss Willard remarked she herself could not afford to be so transparent.

Within a year, the Willards were aroused to the seriousness of the war. Frank and Mary were busy now with war work. There was as yet no Red Cross. Local agencies dealt with the sick and wounded, and cared for families left without a breadwinner. Of Chicago's one hundred thousand inhabitants, fifteen thousand enlisted during the four years. Through two Sanitary Fairs a fund of half a million dollars was raised. This was woman's work. Men drove new McCormick reapers and invented other machinery to speed up food production, built stockyards, multiplied railroads. If Frank read the papers — as of course she did — she must have become aware of the appalling increase in gambling, crime and prostitution, due to war. But no one thought of it as woman's work to deal with these. To scrape lint, to attend war meetings, to pray for the freedom of the slaves, to raise money for soldiers and their families — these were woman's work.

In the spring, Frank and Mary Bannister taught the Evanston school, now grown to two rooms. The work was tremendous — sixteen classes to a teacher, covering the whole field of elementary and high-school subjects! But Frank was glad to be of use. She played ball with her children and spelled them down, and was happy. Happy in spite of the fact that Mary was ill again. On May 30, 1862, she wrote, "Every day school grows pleasanter. . . . My pupils like me, too, I think."

Nine days later, Mary died. Only those who have relinquished their dearest can feel the poignancy of Frank's words: "*Mary is dead*. I write the sentence — stop and look at it — do not know what it means." That was to be at bottom of all her thoughts for months to come, cropping out continually in her journal. All the entries begin and end with Mary.

A month after Mary's death Oliver and Mary Bannister were married and went to Denver to live; Mrs. Willard went East; Mr. Willard took a room in Chicago. Swampscott was closed; Forest Home was sold. To Frank Professor offered the chair of natural sciences, and she returned to the college, "scene of my girlish escapades." She pictures her first Sunday evening as professor — in the parlor after tea, the girls gathered around the piano, kind old Father and Mother Jones, Professor's parents, looking on contentedly, their three handsome sons — two on furlough, and "spiritual-faced Professor with his wife and children, soon to start for China, where Professor has been appointed consul." And she adds: "Professor did not die, as we all thought he would last winter. Mary, my sister Mary, who went with me to see him in his illness, took that longest of all voyages in his stead."

Her twenty-third birthday comes and goes, unnoticed even

by her mother. The omission gives her a queer sensation. She is working too hard. She breaks under the strain. When Lincoln sets the slaves free, it strikes in her heart " a chord that gives out music." Soon life is again stale.

Conscientious as she was, and much as she loved her girls, to be in Evanston without Mary and without a home was more than Frank could bear. On the advice of Bishop and Mrs. Simpson she was released to Pittsburgh Female College. She stayed there a year. She had " changed the spot but not the pain." Thoughts of Mary were ever present. She spent her leisure writing a little book which she called *Nineteen Beautiful Years,* the story of Mary's life, built on Mary's journal. Bishop Foster, past president of Northwestern University, says in the Introduction: " It is the secret history, naïvely recited to itself, of a wonderful soul struggling up through the weaknesses and bewilderments that encompass this life, to the pure, calm and unclouded brightness of eternal day."

The extracts from Mary's journal begin with her eighteenth year, the year of her graduation from college. Some read like passages from St. Francis. Some bubble over with mirth, revealing the " merry saint " of college days. For example: " As I was quietly sewing up in my room today, mother's voice sounded through the hall, ' Mary, come down; I have something for you.' So, with much alacrity, I descended to her room. And what do you suppose she had the kindness to bestow on me? Nothing more nor less than a dose of cod-liver oil! Nothing but a dose, did I say? What can be worse or more heartsickening? . . . Oh, may I never remember the taste of it, and may speedy destruction seize on the rest of it in the long yellow bottle! " Sometimes she takes to narrative, and two events move her deeply in this last year of her life — the wreck of the *Lady Elgin* and the outbreak of war.

The former was one of the worst tragedies that ever befell on the Great Lakes. Of it she writes: " The steamer *Lady Elgin,* bound from Chicago to some northern port, and carrying three hundred passengers, was wrecked during a violent storm, two or three miles from here. Three-fourths of the entire number on board were lost. . . . All day long the waves have been bearing to the shore the lifeless forms of those very dear to someone somewhere." Those still alive were rescued. Students — Oliver among them — did heroic work as life-savers.

Mary seems to have been more alive to the suffering entailed by war than Frank. " Think," she writes, " of the thousands of men living at home in peace today who must fall . . . every man of them somebody's husband or father, somebody's brother or son. . . . I thought, ' Will my brother, my only brother, go to the war? ' Somebody's brother must go, and why not ours? Who are we that our hearts should not be broken? "

A war meeting is held in the Methodist church, and soon even the tenderhearted Mary is fired with war hysteria: " When the ' Star Spangled Banner ' was sung . . . I was half-wild with enthusiasm, though I stood there so quietly." The call comes for volunteers to sign the muster roll: " Rapidly they went: young men whom we all know . . . students . . . men who had wives and daughters looking after them . . . beardless boys with their slight forms and flushed young faces. Cheer after cheer went up from the excited audience as each one took the pen and wrote his name. . . ." But she saw, too, the aftermath: " Oh, if we could have known the agony that will result from what was done . . . we should have filled the house with sobs." She mentions the raising of a community fund for the families left without a wage-earner, and was proud to have Frank subscribe money of her own.

Mary, like her sister, was fond of figures of speech, some fantastic, some merely poetic: "God is like an electric battery. Christ first receives the shock; then come the angels; humanity completes the chain. So the spark of divinity thrills along the line." Again: "Night, the kind old nurse, whose head is gray with moonlight, and who tenderly puts the tired to sleep." All very girlish, but revealing a gentle soul who deeply influenced Frances Willard. Often, to the end of her life, Frank recalls something Mary said or did.

March 5, 1862. Just four years since the girls came to Evanston. Mary writes, "This is my birthday anniversary. I am nineteen. The future looks dark to me. I make no plans."

Still there is no intimation that the end is near, though she says more and more often, "I am so tired!" Frank, who is at home, reads to her, sings to her, talks of the days at Forest Home. With a slate (easy to hold) Mary amuses herself sketching, but her hands tremble and the lines "won't come straight." She notes her father's face as he feels her hot cheeks. Her cough grows more violent. Her rings fall off. "Let Frank wear them till I get well," she says. "Take me to Forest Home," she begs. . . .

They must tell her she is dying.

"Shall I pray?" asks Frank.

"Yes — thankful prayers," Mary whispers.

A message to Oliver and Mary; one to her Sunday school class. "Tell everybody to be good." Then, "Take me, dear Lord!"

Her father lays her head back upon the pillows, with the prayer, "Lord Jesus, receive her spirit!" With gratitude for the happiness she has brought them, they give her back to God.

❁ ❁ ❁ ❁ (VI) ❁ ❁ ❁ ❁

Barn-door Wishes Come True

THE NEXT NINE YEARS BROUGHT MANY CHANGES OF MOMENT in Frances' life — changes unforeseen on that cheerless Sunday long ago, when, standing in the barn door at Forest Home, she had cried in one of her rare fits of discouragement, " I wonder if we shall ever know anything, see anybody, or go anywhere! "

She taught (when she longed to write books), moving often and getting from each change of scene a new viewpoint with added maturity. Pittsburgh with its mountains, mines and foundries was quite unlike her prairie state: the one conservative, the other progressive. Here she began wearing glasses — no trivial change. But the old loneliness dwelt with her. Glad as she was — heartily glad — that she had not " perjured " herself the year she wore a ring, she longed for someone who could be everything to her.

In Pittsburgh Female College she first showed her gift as a speaker in an address to the alumnae. Two years later she was asked to deliver the Commencement address, but declined on the ground that that was not woman's work. Yet only four years later she was to speak in Centenary Church, Chicago, for more than an hour — " without notes," she adds exultantly, with pride in her progress.

That year Mr. Willard built in Evanston a new home now known as " Rest Cottage," a future " mecca for pilgrim feet," as Willis Abbot puts it. Here the woman who had once thought that the public platform was not for her sex was to live as one of the nineteenth century's most persuasive orators. Not being a seer, Frank kept on teaching. Yet from this time on everything she did seems to have counted in building a foundation for her future. Far from least in importance was her experience as secretary of the Methodist Ladies' Centenary Association, a group formed to finance a new building for Garrett Biblical Institute. This association, she says, was one of the first to organize women in a large way. It taught her how to organize women on a vastly larger scale.

Genessee Wesleyan Seminary, at Lima, New York, probably did more for her than any other school outside Evanston. As the oldest seminary of the Methodist Church, it had linked with its history many prominent churchmen: Henry J. Raymond, founder of the *New York Times;* Orange Judd, editor of the *Prairie Farmer;* Joseph Cummings, future president of Northwestern University. The seminary was coeducational, a fact that pleased champions of equality of the sexes.

Here Frances was installed as preceptress of girls. Her new friend Kate Jackson had accompanied her to become teacher of French. Shortly after her arrival Frank was surprised and delighted when an older woman teacher kissed her and exclaimed, "You dear little kitten!" Students laughed incredulously when told that Miss Willard was a teacher. She soon found it no small undertaking to be elder sister to a hundred and eighty girls.

In November a new national holiday was inaugurated. President Johnson proclaimed November twenty-ninth a day of national thanksgiving. Frank wrote: "Thirty-six millions of people at once offering their thanks to the Source of Life and all that comes through living!" What exuberance in those words, "all that comes through living!"

The most exciting event of the year was hearing Horace Greeley speak. It added spice to the occasion to recall his letter of reprimand to the girls who had asked for his autograph.

But the real significance of the Greeley meeting lay in its being Frances' first (recorded) experience in a "motley crowd" carrying banners with slogans. These read, "Down with the One-Man Power!" "Congress Must and Shall Be Sustained!" "Andy Johnson Swinging Around the Circle!"

She liked Greeley's "quiet, unwritten face. . . . Life hasn't hurt him much, the noble old philosopher. I liked to watch him standing there in his nice black suit with velvet vest, wide collar, and queer ruffles of white whiskers; with his bald head, ring on third left-hand finger, and red bandana in his hand. He embodies well the idea of our government — 'Give everybody a fair chance, and let the outcome come!'" The daring of such a program appealed to her. Nothing venture, nothing have.

But again, as so often before, when the novelty of her work wore off the term grew dreary and monotonous.

Mr. Willard had accompanied his daughter and Kate Jackson to Lima, had helped them hang pictures, and had stayed till they were settled. But as he held out his hand in good-by to Frances (apparently there was no kissing) he had turned his head aside as if to hide unwonted tears. The remembrance troubled his daughter as she watched him walk away — "so gentlemanly and tall, but so slight and fragile."

When she returned home the following summer he was in the last stages of tuberculosis. That winter he died at Churchville, at his brother Zophar's, amid old scenes and what friends remained after twenty-seven years. His wife, his daughter and Kate Jackson were at his bedside.

A delegation from Evanston and Chicago met their train a long way from home, to furnish an escort of honor. A Christian gentleman, a man of intellect and integrity, Mr. Willard would be sadly missed in civic and business affairs.

While public honors are being paid him, Frank relives bit by bit their life together — his companionship with his children, his pride in their achievements, his tolerance and sense of fair play, his tenderness during Mary's illness, his letters of encouragement, so original in their wit. Never was he more adorable than that day at the Matteson House, when she was so tongue-tied at sight of the white-clad waiters that she could not give her order. She sees again the twinkle in his eye as he orders for her. She recalls the parcel she opened at Kankakee, to find a book, and "belt-fixings," his letter explained, "such as all the girls are wearing now," and — his own watch! Parting with it he acknowledged was like losing an eye. But Frances needed a watch; neither he nor she had money to buy one (the panic had hit him hard and her salary was small). What else could he do than send his? She recalls his years of service to the college as treasurer. Professor — now on his way home from China — will miss him. . . .

Mrs. Willard, Frank and Kate settled down in Rest Cottage. But not for long. At Lima Kate had talked much of going abroad and taking Frank with her. Mr. Jackson would gladly pay her expenses for the sake of giving his motherless Kate a companion. Mrs. Willard insisted Frank must not miss the opportunity; she would rent Rest Cottage and go to live with Oliver and Mary at Appleton, Wisconsin, where Oliver was now selling insurance.

So on May 23, 1868, Kate and Frank sailed for Europe. At the dock Mr. Jackson waved them his last good-by. Before their return he would have sailed on that journey from which there is no return. Their itinerary would take them north to Finland, east to the Volga, Syria, and Palestine, south into Nubia, and west to the Atlantic seaboard again, where they would study for some time in Paris. The little girl who had felt rebellious at the isolation of farm life had "learned something" and "met people." Now she was "going somewhere." Her three barn-door wishes had come true.

Imagine these two American women in their twenties, in a day when few Americans went abroad, setting out alone, ready to enjoy everything to the full. The first entry in Frank's journal at sea pictures her with her head against the side of the berth, dipping ink from a wineglass furnished by the stewardess. "Let me lie still," she warns; "let me keep this saucy diaphragm in equipoise." The second entry, made at Queenstown, sketches the quaint shops, the little donkeys, the rollicking jaunting cars, and two girls beside themselves with glee. They were to spare no expense.

They saw for the first time palaces, museums, picture galleries — "fine things in their places." They contrasted these with the "emptiness" at home. Then one day their Irish guide said: "America's a country where they'll give a well doing man a chance. We all know that, and we'd go there on our hands and knees, only for the water being in the way." Well, what, after all, were museums, palaces and picture galleries, thought Frank, in comparison with a land of opportunity for a man who wants a chance?

The racy narrative covers many pages of the autobiography. Evidently the carefree life of youth was pleasant to recall on the battlefield of maturity. Most of the travel incidents, however, do not concern this story of how a leader evolved. Two or three entries only are significant in revealing that evolution.

The first has to do with the climb up the Simplon Pass to the Monastery of St. Bernard. As she walked with the men of the party (the other women rode mules) Frank recalled the story in McGuffey's *Third Reader* of Napoleon's question whether he could march thirty thousand men over this pass into Italy in May, while the snow still lay deep. "Can it be done?" he asked.

"It may not be impossible, but —"

"Move forward the legions!" rang his command.

Often in the years to come Frances Willard was to face a strategic situation. "Is it possible?" she would ask.

"Possible, perhaps, but —"

"We'll try it!" would come her swift decision.

The second incident reveals the same persistence she had shown in training her heifer to the saddle. It was at the pyramid of Cheops, which she had set out to climb. Others' failures only whetted Frank's determination. She measured again with her eye the three-and-a-half-foot slabs. Then, grasping the hands of the two Bedouins above and feeling the lift of the Egyptian behind, she mounted the first gigantic step. She graphically compares the climb to stepping from the floor to the top of the bureau, not once but a hundred times, and all in fourteen minutes! The Bedouins said "Yankee Doodle" — meaning Frank — had "Arab feet."

She reached the top more dead than alive, but three minutes later she sat coolly watching the arrival of the men of the party, purple and wheezing as she had been. In silence they looked out together over the vast panorama of tombs. The charm of evening, the zest of novelty, the spice of danger — how she loved them all!

Rome, which appalled her with its dirt and misery, awoke in her a new feeling, "a tender pity for my race." Later, the sight of American slums would fan that pity to white heat.

Her letters home bubble with happiness. Her only anxiety is for her mother. She senses that all is not right with Oliver. "Burn all letters no one else should see," she cautions. As for herself, she still dreams of being a writer. Edward Eggleston has sold some of her articles. When her career as a writer is fairly launched, she and her mother will settle down in a quiet home. For years she cherished that hope.

Oliver is made head of the Chicago branch of the Asbury Insurance Company, and he and his family move into Rest Cottage with his mother. Now Frank's mind is at rest. Thought of the expense Kate is at for her makes her work diligently. From Florence she writes, "I was never such a student as since I came abroad." After the daily lesson in Italian, the afternoon of study and sight-seeing, they spend their evenings talking French and Italian with the cosmopolitan family at the pension.

At Florence word reaches them of the death of Kate's father. Shall they go home? Of what avail, now he is gone? Rather, they will carry out the plans of which he had approved.

While attending lectures at the Sorbonne, it occurred to Frank that she, too, might lecture. Being the woman she was, she had been studying the status of women in the several countries visited. Why not prepare herself to champion a wider world for women? Once a professor had said to her father, "Brother Willard, you may as well give in first as last. The woman question is upon us, and has come to stay."

Her two years abroad gave Frances Willard a broader culture, a sound appreciation of the arts, and a familiarity with French and Italian. More than that, they made her international-minded. The struggle of the masses everywhere for a bare subsistence forced upon her consciousness problems the solution of which seemed always to be in terms of woman — *woman free to promote justice.*

Within a year of her return Frances found herself again installed in the college to which she had come as a student thirteen years before. In 1862 she had come back as professor of natural sciences. Now she came as president — the first woman to be president of a college — not, however, the Northwestern Female College. That institution had had its day and given place to what women meant to fashion after a new model.

Women had proved in war activities their ability as executives. Stimulated by Florence Nightingale's successes in peacetime, women like Susan B. Anthony, Mary A. Livermore and Mrs. A. H. Hoge had graduated from war work into the cause of the emancipation of women. Under like stimulus, Evanston women agitated the idea of founding a woman's college with women trustees, a faculty of women, and a woman president! To be sure, Evanston already had a perfectly good woman's college with a stronger faculty than ever before. But that faculty was only a source of irritation: President Jones, who had once engaged women only, had since his return from China engaged a number of men, when — as everyone ought to know — women understood best the kind of "higher education" girls should have.

In June, 1868, Dr. E. O. Haven accepted the presidency of Northwestern University on condition that women be admitted on the same terms as men. As president of the University of Michigan, he had made provision for coeducation there, though it would not go into effect till 1870. Northwestern, by inaugurating the policy at once, would become the first coeducational university in America, since Oberlin — coeducational since 1834 — was only a college. To be sure, Northwestern was only a college as yet, save in name. But the time was rapidly approaching when it would begin its long projected expansion.

Here, then, were three institutions which threatened to become competitors — a woman's college staffed partly by men, a women's college staffed wholly by women, and a coeducational college aiming to be a university, if panics and wars would ever give it a fair chance. All the promoters of the new college, which they called the Evanston College for Ladies, were old friends of President Jones. They wished to be fair to him, while at the same time keeping true to their new vision of womanhood. Dr. Haven and Professor conferred often on the problem.

Affairs were progressing hopefully toward a solution when Mrs. Willard, Frank and Kate reopened Rest Cottage, which had been closed since Oliver had moved into a home of his own. One day, when Frank was tacking down carpet, Mrs. Kidder, an old neighbor and a trustee of the new college, came over. For a while she watched the capable fingers, the firm-set mouth. Then she said, "Frank, I'm ashamed of you! Let someone else tack down that carpet, and do you take charge of our college."

"Very well," answered Frank laughing. "I was only waiting to be asked." And there ended for a time all thoughts of being a lecturer to emancipate women.

President Jones was greatly pleased when he heard the announcement that Frances E. Willard would be president of the Evanston College for Ladies. He had read the writing on the wall. His day had passed. A new day had dawned. But his Female College should not die; rather, it should be reincarnated.

At the Commencement in 1871 he transferred not only the charter of the old college to the trustees of the new, but its history and its alumnae. The Evanston College for Ladies was to incorporate these as its own. Mrs. Mary Bannister Willard received them on behalf of the trustees, and praised his magnanimity. Dr. Haven said, "He gives up the hope of a lifetime that the educational interests of Evanston may be unified."

But Professor was happy in the assurance that, with Frank as president and Mary Bannister Willard and other old friends on the board, the traditions of the Northwestern Female College would live on.

The immediate need, the board knew, was money for their building. Led by Mrs. Hoge, who had headed at least one Sanitary Fair during the war, the women of Evanston united to make the "Woman's Fourth of July" a grand success. Miss Willard prepared a circular setting forth the purpose of the college, which was now "to supplement the advantages of Northwestern University." In other words, its wings had already been clipped; it was to be only a forerunner of Barnard and Radcliffe.

All summer President Willard canvassed the country, speaking on behalf of the new institution. All summer she planned courses and enrolled students, till the old Female College (which the women had leased till their own building should be finished) was filled. By fall the enterprise was fairly launched, with every promise of success.

Yet there was a tinge of sadness in the letter Frank wrote about this time to Kate Jackson's sister, Mrs. Whitely, on the birth of her first child: "What different worlds we have drifted into, dear Carrie, since those brief, delightful days at Lima, in which we learned to care for one another! You into the sure, safe haven of home; I out upon the wide, wide sea of a 'career' (for such it will be, whether brilliant or not). You into the sweet and mystical relations of wife and motherhood; I into the gentle, fitful friendship of a hundred schoolgirls. You into loving service for husband and child; I into earnest, ceaseless work for the daughters of a thousand homes, who shall yet be happier and wiser because of my toil.

"Who shall say which of us has best fulfilled the will of

Rest Cottage

Frances Willard as Dean of Women,
Northwestern University, 1873

heaven, or best served the needy cause of our common humanity? My cheerful and contented thought is this: Each of us, in her natural place, is working out the bidding of that unseen, benign and loving Spirit that pervades the universe, and whose wondrous adaptation of countless intelligences to their fitting tasks is the greatest proof of his omniscience."

No one who knew her could doubt that, had the choice been hers to make, Frances Willard would have chosen wifehood and motherhood. As it was, her life was to be given to making safer, better homes for other women. Protection of the home was to be the keynote to all her future activities.

Contrary to the original plans of its women founders the Evanston College for Ladies did not stand alone. From the outset it was linked with the university, and the connection became closer each year. Girls ready for college entered university classes; those preparing for college enrolled in the University Preparatory School. Only such as wished to pursue the "more womanly" branches — modern languages, music, art, home economics, hygiene — enrolled at the College for Ladies. So, at the very beginning of her administration, the college president lost much of her authority. As dependence on the university increased, she lost even the title "president" and became "dean."

Circumstances forced this change of plan. A month after the institution opened its doors, the Chicago fire swept away fortunes and nullified pledges on which depended the erection of a college building. Two years later came the panic of '73, ushering in a long period of depression. Financially the College for Ladies was ruined. At this juncture, the university came to its aid, assuming all its debts and appropriating fifty thousand dollars to complete the building. And now, having surrendered all its property rights, the woman's board of fifteen became a shadow of itself.

In her *Glimpses* Miss Willard devotes considerable time to this period, which she had entered upon with high hopes. To her, education meant the ability to meet life successfully, and a prime factor in that progress was the development of self-reliance and self-control. For that, she counted much on her system of self-government. To the Woman's Congress she explained the underlying idea figuratively thus: "I open a 'Character Bank,' in which the 'deposit' is reputation," which might accumulate or be drawn upon. And again, more literally: "I would organize a school as the national government is organized, . . . and would make the discipline of our young people's formative years a direct preparation and rehearsal for their participation in the government of their country later on."

Her purpose was to "reward merit with privilege." Those who were loyal to the regulations were invested with certain powers and responsibilities in governing the hall, and had their names inscribed on the roll of honor. The next promotion was to the ranks of the Self-Governed, who were exempt from all regulations except the preservation of college morale. Their greatest reward, says one of them, was the close association with the dean. Herein lay the secret of the whole plan's success. It was not the rewards of merit, but the personality of the dean, that gave the system prestige. The same charm that was to win thousands of older people to the cause of total abstinence and woman suffrage prompted hundreds of girls to give their full measure of devotion. "Let's see how long we can live without rules!" the dean would say at the beginning of a term, and the response would be immediate. Flagrant offenders were sent home. This was not a reform school. The dean always found time for intimate talks with the lonely or wayward; her sympathy and understanding led many a girl to tell " the history of her life."

Miss Willard's policies worked amazingly well — as long as she was dean of women only. But as university professor she encountered difficulties with the men students. What! Men taught by a woman? Who ever heard of such a thing? Her freshman class of seventy boys set themselves to make life miserable for her. One wrote on the board, " Miss Willard runs the freshmen like a pack of girls." She did not see the legend as she erased the board for class work. Another put a howling cat into her desk. She let it howl the entire hour, deaf to its bedlam. The last endurance test was a squeaking door, swollen by damp weather. A dozen tardy boys, each just one minute later than the last, swung it open — slowly . . . then, slowly . . . closed it. Still that woman professor made no comment. No use! She'd won! Long after, when about to address an audience of five thousand, she laughingly commented that numbers could not disconcert any woman who had taught freshman boys at Northwestern.

While she had been winning popularity among students, her popularity had grown also among the townspeople. In spite of her professional responsibilities she found time to indulge her love of literature and the arts in small clubs — the Shakespeare Club, the Music Club, the Oriental and Greek Club — to each of which she contributed her fresh personality. She hungered for intellectual pursuits.

Before the experiment in coeducation had become well unified Dr. Haven resigned as president of the university to become secretary of the board of education of the Methodist Church. Charles H. Fowler, D.D., who succeeded him, was a man of quite different caliber. Dr. Haven was diplomatic, a scholar and an educator; Dr. Fowler was aggressive, self-centered, and inexperienced in education. He was altogether the wrong running mate for Frances Willard. It helped matters not at all that it was his ring she had worn "three-quarters of a year," and that all Evanston knew it.

Nevertheless, for a time things ran smoothly, on the surface at least. In the university buildings, as in the town, gas supplanted kerosene; a telegraph line established communication between buildings; electric bells rang the change of classes. Northwestern was quite up to date. Under President Fowler, one professional school after another was added. Dean Willard was made professor of aesthetics, and Dr. Frank Bristol, one of her students, compares her classroom to a flower bed (whatever that may mean). But events were shaping to force her out of the garden onto a battlefield.

President Fowler's improvements were substantial. But the improvements did not extend to relations between the university and the college. He and the dean differed radically as to her system of government and as to the woman's board. He would have but "one board, one management." Shorn of all authority, the dean found that her only course was to resign. The townspeople generally sided with her; men students, faculty, and trustees supported President Fowler.

The dean, however, at her own request was granted the opportunity to state her case before handing in her resignation. She herself describes the scene of her apologia in the chapel: in the foreground, trustees, faculty, and reporters; farther back the ousted women trustees of the college and the officers of the Educational Aid Association; behind them, the girls — dearer to her than they knew, for in them she had seen the nucleus of a more gifted womanhood, trained to lead the way into "a wider world for women." She still had visions of that world.

. . . Having read her defense, the already doomed dean and Miss Jackson withdrew.

That night the girls heard their dean weeping. She who had wept only when death took one of her family, now mourned the death of her dearest hopes.

Looking back on that heartbreaking experience, Miss Willard puts its significance thus: " Instead of peace, I was to participate in war. Instead of enjoying the sweetness of home, I was to become a wanderer. Instead of libraries, I was to frequent halls and railway cars. Instead of scholarly and cultured men, I was to see the dregs of saloon and gambling house and haunt of shame." The remaining twenty years of her life she was to fight, says Willis Abbot, for " good government and right living," as the " foe of corruption, whether social or political." In 1874, however, that destiny was still hidden in the lap of the gods, though she had glimpsed it in Paris six years before.

After nursing for months the bitterness bred of a sense of the injustice done her, she took the advice of a man she honored, called on all toward whom she felt unkindly, asked pardon for anything she had done amiss, and said she trusted they would be friends again. The result, she says, was sometimes humorous, sometimes pathetic. When the time came to call on Dr. Fowler she insisted Oliver go with her. Reluctantly he yielded. Approaching the president, she offered her hand, apologized, and asked to be friends. Taken aback, he recovered sufficiently to apologize in turn. She went home buoyant. " Nor do I know," she says, " nor ever mean to know . . . a reason why any human being should hesitate to speak to me with cordiality and kindness."

In *A Classic Town* she sketches three presidents of Northwestern. To Dr. Haven and Dr. Cummings she gives the meed of warm devotion. To Dr. Fowler she pays tribute in a sentence — "a remarkable and famous man" — then quotes from an encyclopedia for the rest of her picture.

Later she was to see that an institution planned to be an independent woman's college could not fit into the scheme of a man's university without friction.

One of the pleasantest associations that resulted from her deanship was election to Alpha Phi sorority in 1875 and serving as its national president in 1888.

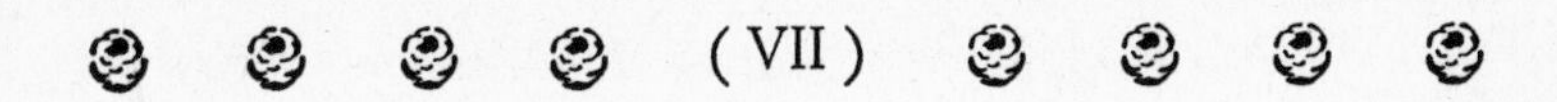

The Opening Way

IT WAS A FAR CRY BACK TO THE DAY WHEN LITTLE FRANK HAD picked out the words of her father's temperance certificate on the dining-room wall, or the day when she had pasted the childish pledge in the family Bible and demanded that all the family sign — and Oliver had marked with crosses the two drinks he would not renounce, cider and beer. It was a long time since, sitting at her mother's knee, she had listened with childish curiosity to one of the rare arguments between her parents.

Her father had told of the new prohibition law in Maine, and added, "I wonder if we shall ever have such a law in rum-cursed Wisconsin."

Only half understanding, she had heard her mother's answer: "Not till women vote." And her father's teasing question, "And how, pray, do you propose to get the vote for women?"

For a moment no answer. Then Mrs. Willard's slow reply, "Like Paul I say, 'You who have put us into prison must take us out.'" A queer answer! But the Bible was full of sayings the child could not understand, and Paul she knew was in the Bible.

No more was said about temperance till the family was discussing the girls' going to Evanston instead of returning to Milwaukee. Someone — perhaps Cousin Morilla — mentioned as a point in favor of Evanston the clause in the university charter forbidding the sale of liquor within four miles of that institution, while Milwaukee was famous for its beer.

Again a long lapse, when teetotalism was taken for granted

in the Willard home. Until 1863, when the Temperance Alliance was formed in Evanston, Frank had read but one article, heard but one lecture on temperance. She was then twenty-four.

Ten years more passed. Then the Woman's Temperance Crusade in Hillsboro, Ohio, woke the country to consciousness of the ruin caused by drink. That Dean Willard was aroused was apparent in the new themes for compositions she suggested to her classes: "John B. Gough," "Neal Dow," "Is Prohibition a Success?" She was outraged when Chicago women narrowly escaped being mobbed after presenting a petition asking for enforcement of the Sunday-closing ordinance. As enthusiasm for temperance grew, she was persuaded to speak in its behalf, first in a Methodist, then in a Unitarian church. Unaccustomed to addressing large audiences, she read her argument. The audiences were polite but lukewarm. "A schoolgirl essay!" she heard someone say. It stirred her fighting blood; she never read again. She had passed her novitiate.

Till she resigned as dean, however, she had no thought of devoting herself to what was called "gospel temperance," much as the altruism and drama of the Hillsboro Crusade had appealed to her, when women of wealth and position had sought men out in saloons in the hope of saving them. Now she was free, she decided to investigate the movement, see the leaders at work, and determine whether to join them. At Old Orchard Beach, Maine, she conferred with General Neal Dow, "Father of the Maine Law," with Mrs. L. M. N. Stevens, already leader of Maine women, and with Francis Murphy, once a saloonkeeper, now a lecturer for temperance. All these struck her as "practical" reformers. In Boston she called on Dr. Dio Lewis, who had kindled the Woman's Crusade in Hillsboro with his prophecy that women could close saloons if they would.

On the way home she stopped off at Pittsburgh to visit her friends at the college. She promptly shocked them by her enthusiasm for the Crusade and her desire to meet Pittsburgh leaders, who were still carrying on, though elsewhere the movement had subsided. Was this the Frances Willard they had associated with everything cultural? Politely they furnished an escort to Crusade headquarters, where she at once joined an outgoing band, and saw — for the first and the last time, she says — the inside of a saloon.

As the crusaders lined up along the curb so as not to disturb traffic, one of the women sang "Jesus the Water of Life Will Give." Says Miss Willard: "It was a novel spectacle. There stood women of undoubted religious devotion and the highest character, most of them crowned with the glory of gray hairs; most of the men raised their hats in passing; even the newsboys touched their caps to the fine ladies." The first saloonkeeper refused them entrance. The second admitted them. Miss Willard looked around her with some curiosity — at the bar, at the barrels pointing their spigots toward the customers, the shelves glittering with glasses and decanters, the floor sprinkled thickly with sawdust. The fumes sickened her.

But the leader laid her Bible on the bar and read a psalm; they sang a hymn; then someone asked Miss Willard to pray, while they knelt in the sawdust, "hard-looking" men all around them. And she prayed as never before save at Mary's deathbed. "This," says she, "was my Crusade baptism."

Meanwhile many schools offered her positions for the coming year. Among them was Dr. Van Norman's fashionable school for young ladies in New York. In the same mail came an urgent appeal from Mrs. Louise S. Rounds to come home and head the infant temperance movement in Chicago.

She weighed the two offers. One meant comradeship, love, and social connections she valued; the other meant isolation, ridicule, social ostracism. The one promised comparative ease; the other poverty and privation, for it could pay no salaries. How, then, was she to support her mother? She recalled the passage she had chanced upon in a hotel: "Trust in the Lord and do good, and verily thou shalt be fed." That settled it. She would live by faith. There was, perhaps, another motive she would not yet acknowledge even to herself, which turned her face toward temperance.

She had declined a twenty-four hundred dollar salary — huge for a woman in that day — as lady principal, a position of dignity, to become president of the Chicago Temperance Union and leader of a forlorn hope. Friends advised against it. Kate Jackson protested. Bishop Simpson, champion of woman's rights, said frankly that, with a mother to support, she could not afford such a luxury as philanthropy. Mrs. Mary A. Livermore alone advised the step. The Willards were no less astounded than others at her choice. But Frank knew her own mind; she had deliberated three months. Oliver, who had now become editor of a Chicago paper, quietly assumed the added burden, though he had a family of six to support. Fortunately his mother owned her home.

To test her faith the new president concealed from the Union the fact that she had no income. She even refused to let money be raised for her salary. Other enterprises had been supported by faith. She held fast to the promise she should "be fed."

"So," she says, "with no financial backing whatever, I opened the first headquarters known to the Woman's Christian Temperance Union annals, the Young Men's Christian Association giving me a room rent-free; organized committees for the few lines of work then thought of by us; started a daily three o'clock prayer-meeting at which signing the pledge and seeking the Lord behind the pledge were constant factors; sent articles and paragraphs to the local press, having called on every editor in town and asked his help or at least his tolerance; addressed Sunday schools, ministers and mass meetings, and once in a while made a dash into some town or village, where I spoke, receiving a collection, which represented financially my little all."

For several months things ran along smoothly, with Miss Willard as a new St. Francis. Sometimes she went hungry or walked long distances because of an empty purse. She did not regret the experience; it enlarged her sympathy for those who were penniless. Twenty-five years later she looked back on this as the loveliest period of her life. "I communed with God; dwelt in the spirit; this world had nothing to give me, nothing to take away." Her traveling expenses were paid by the Union; usually she was entertained wherever she spoke. But the collections — her little all — were as a rule very, very small. She was poor.

She was busy, too. An excerpt from her notebook reads: "Back from my meeting at ——— and almost frozen. Found two at office trying to help three poor fellows. . . . We have more cases, histories, crises, calamitous distress revealed than could be helped by a millionaire. This work is by far the most blessed of my life . . . good to see the men grow clean and shaved and brightened. . . . My *gospel* talks are in great demand; engagements crowd upon me for *temperance*." Friends urge she give all her time to the former. But she cannot feel that "anything so forlorn as temperance should be deserted by a single adherent." Men sometimes offer to help, but the ladies hold back. They will come sometime, she is sure.

The year before, when she was dean at Northwestern, the Woman's Congress had heard her gladly. This year, as temperance worker, she was no longer welcome. It was whispered that she spoke to railroad men and in the red-light district! She had lost caste. Only Mrs. Livermore's demand secured for her a hearing.

One day Oliver protested: "Frank, your faith method is simply a challenge to the Almighty. You've put a chip on your shoulder, and dared Omnipotence to knock it off." Still, he gave full reports in his paper of what the women were doing.

It was during these first months as a reformer that Miss Willard wrote her old college friend Louisa Dake (now Mrs. Medlar) that on a certain date she would speak in Woodstock, Louisa's home town, and organize a W.C.T.U. there. Would "Louie" see that she had a good audience?

W.C.T.U.? Cabalistic letters to Mrs. Medlar — she hardly knew their meaning. It was enough, however, that Frank wanted her help — Frank, who since her graduation had taught in a dozen or more places, traveled and studied abroad two years, been president of a college, and after this promising beginning had — hidden her talent in a forlorn cause, foredoomed, men said, to failure! Yet this was the same Frank Willard who at college had led in scholarship and popularity; the same convincing speaker in debate; the same wholehearted, unaffected, enthusiastic leader who had sung "Scotland's Burning" in the little brown schoolhouse at Forest Home.

Frank came. Mrs. Medlar found her still the same dynamic person, only now more warming because of her sympathy and ready laugh. She was evidently not taking herself too seriously, though believing unalterably in the invincibility of her cause. Before the meeting Frank looked over the mail that had been following her and remarked nonchalantly, "Mother wants me to come home and see about the taxes. She looks to me to help her out." Not a word about the scarcity of money. But in the mail was also a railway pass which would lighten expenses. More heartening still was to be the ten-dollar collection after her talk. Ten dollars! Why, Galesburg, a much larger place, had given only three dollars.

Presently Frank asked, "How many saloons have you in this town?"

"Seven," answered Louie, wondering what Frank thought she could do about it.

Frank shook her head. "Bad, very bad!" she said slowly. "But" — with assurance — "there needn't be one, if you women had a mind to work."

The church was decorated with apple blossoms and other spring flowers; there were a choir and a brass band. Frank expressed her pleasure as she and Louie walked up the aisle arm in arm.

As she spoke, Louie looked her over. How changed from the girl Louie had once called homely! Her straight figure had taken on elegance, above her oval face was a wealth of light-brown hair; the voice once heavy was now "clear and bell-like." How thrilling seemed her appeal — a "battle-cry," Louie called it, that would be heard the land over, wherever Frank's footsteps led.

Woodstock, like other towns, rallied at the call. The seven saloonkeepers trembled — till they discovered that the women, having organized, didn't know what to do next. Ignorance of legitimate means to oust saloons and fear of being "unwomanly" left that Union, like many others, for the time being ineffectual.

The work grew heavier. She was not robust. While speaking at Freeport, Illinois, she became ill and was hurried home, where she took to her bed with inflammatory rheumatism.

"You'd better call a doctor," she advised her mother.

"No," said Mrs. Willard, "you are going by faith; you do not need a doctor."

Frank knew, however, that this was only a grim joke; that years of doctoring the family at Forest Home had given her mother confidence in her own medical skill.

When she had nursed Frank back to health, Mrs. Willard said one day, "I want you to listen. I believe in faith as much as you do, but you have, with pure intention yet ignorantly, flown into the face of Providence. Those good women spoke to you about a maintenance the very day they chose you president. That was your heavenly Father's kind provision, and you turned away from it and dictated to him the method of his care. . . . God isn't going to start loaves of bread flying down the chimney, nor set the fire going in my stove without fuel. . . . You are out at the elbows, down at the heel, and down sick. Now write those temperance ladies a plain statement of facts. . . ." Her daughter obeyed.

By return mail came a check for a hundred dollars. "And my faith," wrote Miss Willard humorously, "was met upon the heavenly Father's basis, not upon the one I had prescribed for him." But she had enjoyed the episode; she felt richer because of it.

As yet she stood only on the threshold of the most significant period of her life. Two thirds of that life would be forgotten; this last third alone would be remembered — remembered with scorn or gratitude, with love or strong dislike, with understanding or misunderstanding. She weighed well the consequences of crossing that threshold.

Chicago was just then a battlefield between the forces of "puritanism" and those of "personal liberty." The first was represented by the Law and Order League, the other by the

People's party. In 1873 the league had secured Sunday closing not only of saloons, but of the Exposition Building which housed a " wealth " of exhibits from all over the world. In retaliation the People's party was overwhelmingly victorious in the next election; saloons ran wide open on Sunday, and the " working man " could again " enjoy the Exposition on his only free day." The German press, headed by A. C. Hessing, was uncompromisingly against restricting the sale of beer. The Chicago Temperance Union took neither side. It bided its time. It would develop its own methods of combating evil.

Shortly after Miss Willard became president of the Chicago Union, she was made delegate to a convention called by Mrs. Jennie F. Willing at Bloomington to organize a state union. At that convention she publicly dedicated herself to the work of reform. As a hundred women marched, two by two, along the street " under the stars," she felt they marched to victory. She says, " My life had hardly known a more exalted moment. I seemed to see the end from the beginning. And when one has done that, nothing has power to discourage or to daunt." Mrs. Willing was elected state president, Miss Willard state secretary.

In August, Mrs. Willing, with Mrs. Mattie McClellan Brown of Cincinnati and Mrs. Emily Huntington Miller of Evanston, called a national convention of temperance women to meet in Cleveland in November. Women from seventeen states answered the call, and held a three-day session. Mrs. Willing and Miss Willard laid out a plan of work; Mrs. J. Ellen Foster of Iowa presented the constitution. The declaration of principles, including the pledge of total abstinence and the promise to use all legitimate means against the liquor traffic, was written by Miss Willard.

The Woman's Christian Temperance Union was defined as

DECLARATION OF PRINCIPLES

Written by Frances E. Willard

(*Adopted 1874*)

We believe in the coming of His Kingdom whose service is perfect freedom, because His laws, written in our members as well as in nature and in grace, are perfect, converting the soul.

We believe in the gospel of the Golden Rule, and that each man's habits of life should be an example safe and beneficent for every other man to follow.

We believe that God created both man and woman in His own image, and therefore we believe in one standard of purity for both men and women, and in the equal right of all to hold opinions, and to express the same with equal freedom.

We believe in a living wage; in an eight-hour day; in courts of conciliation and arbitration; in justice as opposed to greed of gain; and in " Peace on earth and good will to men."

We therefore formulate, and for ourselves adopt the following pledge, asking our sisters and brothers of a common danger and a common hope, to make a common cause with us, in working its reasonable and helpful precepts into the practice of everyday life:

" I hereby solemnly promise, God helping me, to abstain from all distilled, fermented and malt liquors, including wine, beer and cider, and to employ all proper means to discourage the use of and traffic in the same."

To confirm and enforce the rationale of this pledge, we declare our purpose to educate the young; to form a better public sentiment; to reform so far as possible, by religious, ethical and scientific means, the drinking classes; to seek the transforming power of Divine grace for ourselves and all for whom we work, that they and we may willfully transcend no law of pure and wholesome living; and finally we pledge ourselves to labor and to pray that all these principles, founded upon the gospel of Christ, may be worked out into the customs of society and the laws of the land.

" an organization of Christian women banded together for the protection of the home, the abolition of the liquor traffic, and the triumph of Christ's Golden Rule in custom and in law." At its very inception it declared its belief in the equal rights and responsibilities of men and women; in a living wage, an eight-hour day, courts of conciliation and arbitration; in justice as opposed to greed; in " peace on earth, good will to men." Three ways of discouraging the liquor traffic were suggested: education of the young, reform of drinkers, and " pure and wholesome living " on the part of the Union's members.

A significant act of that first convention was tabling such extreme resolutions as that demanding the disfranchisement of men engaged in the liquor traffic. To set the stamp of disapproval on intolerance, Miss Willard proposed the resolution: " Recognizing that our cause is and will be combated by mighty, determined and relentless forces, we will, trusting in him who is the Prince of Peace, meet argument with argument, misjudgment with patience, denunciation with kindness, and all our difficulties and dangers with prayer." Often in afteryears she had occasion to remind her coworkers of this policy.

The *Temperance Women's Own Paper* (not theirs) announced: " The Woman's Christian Temperance Union of Chicago, . . . has begun a systematic attempt to enlighten and convince the public . . . not by grogshop crusades, but by spreading information concerning the evils of intemperance. . . . Only let the Union be sure of its facts."

A wise admonition. Thus far ridicule had been meted out to a movement looked upon as ephemeral. As it showed evidence of permanence, Miss Willard foresaw that ridicule would turn to enmity, enmity to virulence. The Union must, indeed, be sure of its facts.

This first national convention would have made her president, but she declined on the ground of her inexperience. She did, however, consent to be corresponding secretary, with Mrs. Annie Wittenmeyer of Pennsylvania as president. Such women as Mrs. Wittenmeyer, Mrs. Mary T. Lathrap, Mrs. J. Ellen Foster, Mrs. Zerelda Wallace, and Mrs. Mary T. Leavitt, future leaders and associates, elicited her admiration. She was proud to work with them, but she would not take the lead till she was qualified.

Few of these women could make a speech as yet. For several years indeed W.C.T.U. conventions were not in the least conventional. Someone called them "homelike." But conventional or homelike, they attended strictly to business. Before the second national convention met the corresponding secretary had prepared her *Hints and Helps for the W.C.T.U.*, to facilitate the transaction of business.

Frances Willard as Evanston had known her had been transformed into a person her townspeople didn't quite understand. Says Miss Gordon, her biographer, "She who had studied books, now studied humanity. Delighting in music and art, she gave herself with abandon to scenes the reverse of artistic. . . . For music, she now had gospel hymns . . . sung by men upon whose lips the praises of God were unaccustomed."

But she recognized an open door, beyond which she could put to use her gift as organizer. What she did not recognize was that this organization was to overspread all America, and ultimately the world.

(VIII)

Under a Cloud

For some years — ever since a day in Paris — Frances Willard had been brooding on the thought of a "wider world for women," whom she believed to be the regenerating force in human progress. But not till two years after entering temperance work did she feel the time had come to champion publicly the ballot for woman as a "protection to the home." Home was to her the center of the universe; its protection was her constant theme. To protect the home she became a suffragist.

She presented her case for the first time before the Woman's Congress, then meeting in Philadelphia. The congress that had cold-shouldered her as a champion of total abstinence now locked arms with her again. Elsewhere, however, she was more unwelcome than ever. When, during the Centennial Exposition at Philadelphia in 1876, she asked to speak at the International Temperance convention on "The Home-Protection Ballot for Women," her request was "mildly but firmly" refused. Any other theme but that, said the convention. Even the National W.C.T.U. granted her a hearing only because she was a delegate, and then with great reluctance.

That address, tame as it seems today, kindled fires of indignation. The convention fairly sizzled. She argued that only through woman's vote could the cause of temperance succeed. Women constituted the vast majority of those that could be counted upon to vote against dramshops. Chief sufferers from the liquor traffic, women would favor its prohibition. She told of the conversation between her parents when the Maine law was first passed, and her mother's confidence that "rum-cursed" Wisconsin would have a like law when women could vote.

"Two years of struggle in this temperance reform have shown me my duty," she said, "so clearly and impressively that I long ago passed the Rubicon of silence and am ready for any battle that shall be involved in this honest declaration of the faith that is in me. 'Fight behind masked batteries a little longer!' whisper good friends and true. So I have been fighting hitherto; but it is a style of warfare altogether foreign to my temperament. . . . I must tilt a free lance henceforth on the splendid battlefield of this reform. . . . It is women who have given the costliest hostages to fortune. . . . Give them power to protect those whom they have so loved."

Some who heard her wept, foreseeing the punishment she had brought upon herself. She could feel the icy chill of disapproval. Mrs. Wittenmeyer, with whom she had traveled and worked in perfect harmony for two years, was presiding. But Mrs. Wittenmeyer made it quite clear that the W.C.T.U. was in no wise responsible for the speaker's radical utterances. With dignity she added, "We do not propose to trail our skirts through the mire of politics." And considering the length of the skirts of that day, one shudders at thought of the mire they could accumulate.

As the delegates filed out, a prominent woman walking beside the daring suffragist said sharply, "You might have been a leader in our national councils, but you have deliberately chosen to be only a scout."

Three years later, the convention elected Miss Willard national president; four years later it voted in favor of woman suffrage. But temporarily she was in eclipse.

So it was that, when the following January Dwight L. Moody asked Miss Willard to conduct his meetings for women in the great Chicago Tabernacle, she was free and delighted to accept his offer. To be sure, she was still corresponding secretary for the National W.C.T.U., but that position was not yet onerous. She liked evangelistic work, and had counted much upon the Union's daily gospel meetings for churchless men. But she had been disappointed in having so few women in the audience. She welcomed, therefore, the idea of working with America's leading evangelist in women's meetings.

She admired Moody immensely. He was a Chicago man, who on the salary of a shoe-salesman had established a mission, and finally devoted his entire time to " selling religion," as the less reverent said. Says Lloyd Lewis: " He used to canvass a tough district for ragged youngsters, wash and clothe them, and hurry them to the mission house. That was the sort of man he was." And that was the sort of man Miss Willard liked. He had dedicated his life to " saving souls "; so had she. Frankly, of their two ways of going about it, she liked his better. For she was a born preacher; all her addresses suggest the attitude of the pastor to his flock rather than that of the more impersonal lecturer.

To Mr. Moody she candidly confessed her lack of training in Bible study, but he thought she might, for that very reason, be more effective.

One stormy Sunday, when nine thousand women had gathered to hear Moody, there " surged in " upon her " the mighty significance of such an army of wives and mothers, sisters and daughters." The thrill it gave her was to be a recurring inspiration in days to come. Some weeks later, she introduced John B. Gough, reformed drinker, to the largest temperance audience she ever saw, unless perhaps in an ovation to herself at the height of her career. How magnificently he spoke, while his little wife sat beside him knitting!

Near the end of his Chicago engagement, Mr. Moody sent for his assistant and asked her to accompany him to Boston. When she referred the matter to her mother, the answer came at once, "Enter every open door." Could she foresee how many doors would open to Frank, how many Frank would unlock?

In Boston, Miss Willard was guest in a beautiful home. She gave her forenoons to the Moody meetings, her afternoons to the W.C.T.U. correspondence. Sometimes of an evening she spoke on temperance.

One day Moody said abruptly, "I see by the papers that you are talking temperance all around the suburbs. Why do you do that? I want all there is of you for the Boston meetings."

"I have no money," was her reply. "I must earn some."

"You don't mean that I've given you nothing?" he exclaimed.

"Of course you've given me nothing," said she laughing.

"Who paid your way from Chicago?"

"I did."

"Didn't those fellows" — he named some friends — "send you money for traveling expenses?"

"I guess they forgot it."

"Well! I never heard the like!" And he left her.

That evening she received a "handsome" check, with the injunction, "Don't you go beating about in the suburbs any more!"

Often there were a thousand women at her meetings, occasionally as many as fourteen hundred. When Moody called a temperance conference at which Gough, Wanamaker, and other notables were to speak, Miss Willard was scheduled for what was virtually a sermon. She protested that her ideas might not suit these eastern conservatives. Moody laughed " in his cheery way " and said, " It's just what they need."

But one day they clashed and there was no healing laughter. The National W.C.T.U. convention was to meet at Malden. Miss Willard and Mrs. Livermore were among the speakers. When she told Mr. Moody, he astounded her by refusing to let her speak from the same platform with one who denied the divinity of Christ. She yielded, because of her contract. But when he would have engaged her for another season, she refused, saying, " All my life I have been devoted to the advancement of woman in education and opportunity. . . . I dare not say, 'With you I will speak, . . . with you I will not.' . . . Whosoever will, may work with me."

She did not act hastily. She took all summer to think it over. Ten years after, she wrote with regret of the " wider fields " that would have opened to her through longer association with Moody. But intolerance she could not tolerate. Though Kate Jackson and others tried to dissuade her from re-entering temperance work, with all its social hazards, she turned to it again as to an old friend.

Meanwhile, quietly and unobtrusively, Madam Willard (as she was now called) was exerting an influence in her own community for the advancement of women. Josiah Willard was no longer there to note with quizzical smile what his women folk were doing to upset all his traditions. His daughter was what Edward Everett Hale called " a child of the public." His wife was president of the Evanston W.C.T.U. and a member of the Pro-and-Con Club, a woman's forum founded by Mrs. Elizabeth Boynton Harbert, widely known suffragist. He would have frowned, perhaps, when his wife pointed out the new feature in journalism, "The Woman's Kingdom," which Mrs. Harbert edited in the Chicago *Inter-Ocean*, reaching thousands with stories of woman's achievements. But he would have read it.

He would have seen Evanston full of "strong-minded" women. He might even have overheard the new minister apologize for speaking flippantly of woman suffrage, confessing he had only just become aware that it was an article of faith in that suburb. Josiah might have disapproved of all this, but he would have had to agree with his wife that "human progress must be viewed from the angle of vision made by the eyes of man and woman."

Madam Willard's life radiated helpfulness. Many brought her their problems, their sorrows, their discouragements. She knew the answer or remedy for each. Friends called her their "Gibraltar"; some thought her a greater woman than her daughter. As a girl, Frank had written in her journal: "My nature is so inwoven into hers that I almost think it would be death for me to have the bond severed, and one so much of myself gone over the river. . . . I cling to her more than did ever any other of her children, perhaps because I am to need her more. I am very proud of her, and few women that I have ever known have satisfied me as she does. She has a fine intellect."

The rest of the family went "over the river." Every year Frank had more need of her mother, that wise and dispassionate critic of all the daughter did. When Frank wrote that appraisal, she had seen few women outside the villages of Janesville and Evanston. She was to see thousands, of many nationalities. Women of rank and culture, intellectual women from Europe and the Orient would be her guests. But time, travel and guests would but confirm the judgment of her girlhood.

And now for a year Frances Willard, no longer national secretary of the W.C.T.U., was a free lance. At the suggestion of friends, she signed up with a lecture bureau, and endured for just three weeks the experience of being "personally conducted" day and night. The remembrance never ceased to be amusing: "It was a damper to one of my temperament and habitudes. To go from the genial, breezy, outdoorsy temperance meeting, the warm, tender, exalted gospel meeting, the homelike W.C.T.U. convention, into a human snowball of folks who have 'paid to get in' and are reckoning as one proceeds whether they are going to 'get their money's worth' — is an experience not to be endured with equanimity by one who can slip his head out of its noose. To have a solemn Lyceum Committee of men meet you at the train, take you to a hotel of funereal dreariness; to march upon a stage no woman's hand has beautified; to have no heartsome music or winsome prayer . . . and after you've 'gone through your speech' . . . to hear the jeremiad of the treasurer that they 'hadn't sold so many tickets as they had hoped,' or 'the weather was against them,' or 'counter attractions had proved too powerful' — all this is 'nerve wear' to no purpose."

Worst indignity of all was "to be carted over the country as if you were a case of codfish or a keg of nails. . . . I hope never again to see a 'bureau!'" Doubtless the manager, too, rejoiced, for Miss Willard had refused to have her price raised from twenty-five dollars, even when the bureau could have got three times that amount!

That spring, the spring of 1878, Oliver Willard died suddenly. As editor of the Chicago *Evening Mail* and later of the *Post,* he had done all he could consistently to advance Frank's work. He had been tolerant, though not always seeing eye to eye with her. One of his last acts had been to work up a good audience for her on her first public appearance in Evanston since leaving the university four years before.

The evening came. The audience was all one could ask in size and quality. Madam Willard was there. Mrs. Oliver Willard was there with her four children. But where was Oliver? Not till the meeting was over did word reach them that Oliver lay dangerously ill at the Palmer House in Chicago.

Next day he was apparently better, and urged Frank to keep an engagement in Michigan. Before evening he died. Frank, recalled by a telegram, expected to find her mother crushed, for Oliver was " the pride and darling of her life." Instead, her face was radiant as she said, " Praise heaven! I've grown gray praying for my son; and now, your brother Oliver is safe with God! "

His last words to his wife had been, " Mary, all your prayers for me are answered."

To understand these enigmatic words, one must know more of Oliver's life since he had left Forest Home for college. When, fresh from Beloit, he had entered Garrett Biblical Institute, Evanston had recognized in him the Willard brains and the Willard originality, had discerned that, like his father, he was a man to tie to, a man conservative and honest in word and deed, but more genial than his father. He was not unlike his sister Frank in a certain winsome forthrightness of speech. Popular himself, he had married Mary Bannister, one of the most popular girls in town, his sisters' college chum. Most of the village had seen them off for Denver, in the far-away, little known territory of Colorado, just being organized for statehood. Thither covered wagons were still bearing gold seekers — wagons with the legend, " Pike's Peak or bust."

Word came, now and then, of Oliver as pastor of the first Methodist church in Denver; of Oliver as presiding elder at the unprecedented age of twenty-seven; of Oliver as one of the founders of a coeducational seminary, out of which was to grow the University of Denver. His future looked bright. Suddenly he left Denver and resigned from the ministry. Evanston heard that he had accidentally killed at target practice a child who had run between him and the target. After that, he dropped out of Evanston news till his mother went to be with him and Mary at Appleton during Frank's absence abroad.

Before Frank's return Oliver came back to Evanston. But not the lighthearted, laughing Oliver who had left there nine years before. After the Denver tragedy he had taken to drink — first a little, then a little more, till the habit was fixed. Undoubtedly his sister was thinking of him (whose death she calls " the most significant experience of my life ") when she said of the habit: "I have seen it slowly, imperceptibly wrap men round and round in its close winding-sheet, as if they were Egyptian mummies. . . . They never knew their bondage until the first faint movement toward a better life."

Frequently, says Oliver's son, this onetime home-lover would disappear for days, seeking solace, perhaps forgetfulness. Where he went no one knew. It was during this period of wanderlust that his son Frank was born — Frank, master tramp and ne'er-do-well, whom older readers know by his pen name "Josiah Flynt." Not till a year or two before his death did Oliver conquer temptation and resume his proper place in the community. Mary never left him; together they worked on his paper. She became trained as a journalist.

Now Oliver was gone, but two of the Willards of Forest Home remained.

Soon after Oliver's death Rest Cottage took on new life. Hammers and saws were heard all day at the north end of the house, where the "Annex" was growing to shelter Mary and her brood. There began a closer association than ever between "Mary B." and Frank. Together they would bring up Oliver's children.

The eldest, Katharine, or "Puss," continued to be "little mother" and go to school. But now she could look for aid and advice to "grandma" and to Hannah, grandma's housekeeper. To the younger children, grandma's room was a place of ever new possibilities. Even runaway Frank, aged five, could here become enthralled watching grandma make dolls out of rags and paint on them marvelous faces. As for Puss, it was fun to have tea with grandma and Hannah after school, each in turn asking the blessing; or to watch the ceremony of doughnut making, a responsibility never delegated to Hannah till Madam Willard was too feeble to perform it herself.

Grandma was gentle with the children, for she said they had as yet no experience by which to gauge themselves; they needed encouragement to bring out their best. But she never kissed or fondled them; her caresses, says their mother, were in gently spoken words.

Meanwhile Frances and Mary B. were trying to save the *Post,* Oliver's paper, mortgaged to death, but with a staff of fifty men to be paid every Saturday. Finally it was sold to Victor F. Lawson and Melville E. Stone of the *Daily News*. The women had failed — failure was a foregone conclusion — but the experience was to prove valuable: to Mary as future editor of the *Union Signal,* organ of the W.C.T.U., to Frances for the clearer understanding it gave her of what constitutes news and how to use it. Moreover, the experience clarified her sense of business integrity. The *Post* was running liquor advertisements. She let them run, though she was branded as a traitor to her cause. She could only say in answer to her accusers that these advertisements had been accepted by the former management under contract for a stipulated time. Till that time expired, she felt in honor bound to fulfill her part of the contract. She was making no new contracts of that kind. But censure, even to the point of vituperation, seems not to have affected her prestige with the W.C.T.U.

Most important of the changes that had taken place at Rest Cottage was the coming of Anna Gordon, whom Miss Willard calls " the rarest of my friends — a solace and a support."

One evening during the Moody meetings in Boston, the organist had failed to appear. With some urging, a young woman in the audience had been persuaded to substitute. From that time on she continued as Moody's organist, while between her and Miss Willard developed one of those rare friendships based on perfect understanding. For twenty years they were inseparable. In time Miss Gordon became business manager to her chief. Ultimately, she took over the care of both Willards. Correspondence (long-hand), lecture engagements, callers, social functions — all were managed by her capable hands. Into those same hands Madam Willard let slip, one after another, the responsibilities of homemaker. To Miss Willard the house " became a charming place " as she could afford to improve it. Mrs. Ole Bull and another friend gave money to build a new " Den." Anna Gordon saw to it that there was no mistake in carrying out the specifications. She managed the growing staff of under-secretaries and kept the office running like clockwork.

It was Anna Gordon who bought the materials and engaged the Swedish dressmaker when Madam Willard needed a new straight-line two-piece black dress or Frances must add one or more Jenness-Miller costumes to her wardrobe. It was Anna

Gordon who selected their hats, fitting one to the somewhat heavy but dignified face of the mother, another to the trim stylishness of the daughter.

Anna Gordon arranged all the minutiae of their constant traveling. In her *Glimpses* Miss Willard pays many a tribute to this secretary who was so much more than a secretary. She was, says Frances, " a young woman who understands traveling as Robert Bonner does Maud S. [his famous trotter], and who hasn't her superior as a businesswoman on this continent — I have gone my way in peace since 1878."

Anna planned the entertainment of the guests who came to Rest Cottage — more and more distinguished guests as time went on. Among them none was more charming than Lady Henry Somerset — cultured, witty, wise, yet withal so gentle and considerate that Madam Willard called her " my English daughter." In turn Lady Henry publicly recognized what a factor that mother had been in her daughter's success.

But in 1878 Lady Henry and other distinguished visitors were " beyond the dim unknown."

(IX)

New Openings

THAT FALL MISS WILLARD THREW HERSELF AGAIN, HEART AND soul, into the work of the W.C.T.U., which now showed distinct cleavage into conservatives and liberals. The conservatives, led by Mrs. Wittenmeyer, advocated centralization of power; the liberals, led by Miss Willard, would leave local and state unions to develop along lines determined by local conditions. Woman suffrage was now a subject of lively debate. The conservatives opposed it; the liberals saw in it the only means of winning temperance legislation. With characteristic tolerance, Miss Willard insisted on the right of each member to accept or reject it. Her faction did, however, secure the convention's consent to local unions' reporting in *Our Union* (later the *Union Signal*) what each was doing, if anything, to secure the right of women to vote on local option.

As Illinois president Miss Willard was delegated to present to the state legislature a petition asking that Illinois women be granted the right to vote " wet " or " dry " in their communities. She writes an amusing account of this her first experience as lobbyist. The campaign was conducted after a fashion of her own that must have astounded the conventional politicians with their fondness for red tape. Madam Willard and Anna Gordon had spent many weary hours pasting the sheets of signatures to the petition on a strip of white muslin and binding it with red and blue.

With this petition — it was nearly a quarter of a mile long

— the women decorated the State House. They sang " Home, Sweet Home " in the empty senate chamber; they held prayer meetings in rooms they found vacant and atop the Lincoln Monument; they convened mass meetings throughout the state.

The state geologist turned over to them his room at the State House. They made it homelike with birds and flowers. Townswomen brought their sewing, and doubtless carried their lunch, as Miss Willard did hers. A " good temperance man " carried their cards to legislators who were at leisure. Each was interviewed and opposite his name was set a plus or a minus sign " according to his leaning." The farmers in a body promised their support, but it was hard to find a legislator who would jeopardize his position by presenting their bill.

They got nowhere. Doubtless their methods were too sensational. Miss Willard ascribed their failure to the fact that the beer and whisky interests were nowhere so strongly entrenched as in Illinois, " with Chicago and Peoria as the foci of an ellipse in which our politicians move as in an orbit."

But the sensational campaign was not without value. The men of the state — the only voters — were so aroused that 635 towns out of the 832 which voted on local option that spring went " dry."

The next year (1879) Frances E. Willard, liberal, began her long career as national president. At once things began to hum in the office of the National Woman's Christian Temperance Union. Within a year receipts doubled, though as yet their total was only $2,048. Headquarters were established in New York City — a move that rather takes one's breath when one considers that paltry two thousand dollars. Office efficiency was increased by the installation of up-to-date equipment. The organization was simplified and unified by the substitution of departments for committees. Red tape was eliminated.

" Frances Willard made the temperance movement practical,"

says Willis Abbot; "made what was then the little town of Evanston a mecca for all who believed in *practical reform.*" She demonstrated her practicality in the well ordered machinery of what grew to be a world-wide organization of women. She was quick to recognize talent along any line, "from executive ability to carrying flowers to the sick and those in prison." She was judicious enough to keep finance in the background and to prescribe dues the poorest could pay. Moreover, she kept her little organization free from the "dictation of capitalists, politicians, corporate powers of any kind." Acknowledging no dictation herself, she granted equal freedom to every member. "But she was hard to handle at times," says one — "impossible to handle," he might have said, though Miss Gordon asserts that she was "essentially a harmonizer" in matters of policy. Only when principle was involved did she show herself an uncompromising foe.

But underpinning and fortifying her practical sense was religion — a religion of the body, which should "correlate with Christ's wholesome, practical religion of the soul." To "The kingdom of God is within you" she would give new meaning. "The body is the temple of the Holy Ghost" should no longer seem mystical. "All pure habits, all health and sanity of brain" should make for the kingdom of heaven. "The steady pulse, the calm and quiet thought, the splendid equipoise of will, the patient industry that forges right straight on, and cannot be abashed or turned aside — these make for the kingdom of heaven." It was in this union of religion with civilization that she trusted to save mankind.

At the outset she had laid down as a W.C.T.U. principle, "Only the golden rule of Christ can bring the golden age of man." Hers was not merely a rule that prescribed a duty, but a rule prompted by love. In one of those similes so characteristic of her she said: "No matter how near the water in the boiler comes to being steam, it will not move the locomotive one inch until it *is* steam — that elastic, invisible, irresistible power. Love is like that. . . . Nothing else will ever fuse the hearts of men in those reforms by which the gospel of Christ becomes regnant in the world."

From the time she became national president, Frances Willard was seldom in Evanston, save for the three to five weeks in summer she spent with her mother. Office and speaking engagements filled her days and evenings. She who loved music and art could seldom, if ever, enjoy a concert or an art exhibit; she who had delighted in club meetings could never attend one. She who had feasted on books had no time for reading anything but the news and her correspondence. She who had a "strong natural liking" for the theater turned sadly from it as "not for me."

Old Evanston friends followed her in her activities as set forth in the daily press and — often quite differently — in the W.C.T.U. organ. Many who knew her — perhaps most — questioned the wisdom of the cause she championed. None questioned her sincerity. None loved her the less, even if they thought she was wrong.

The first national convention at which Miss Willard presided was held in Boston in the fall of 1880. That year has been called "the great divide" between the W.C.T.U.'s old and new methods of work. The greatest change is credited to the wit of Mrs. Hannah Whitall Smith. When asked to serve on one of the many standing committees, she replied that the ideal committee was composed of three members of whom one was a permanent invalid, another permanently out of town. Thereupon the twenty standing committees were transformed into twenty departments, each under a superintendent.

In her first annual address, Miss Willard presented a threefold plan to coordinate these departments: 1. The Union had sought the reform of drunkards through gospel meetings, men's clubs and personal appeal. But practical Miss Willard could not let "good impulses and enthusiasm" go to waste for lack of directing. So Mrs. S. M. I. Henry had founded at Lake Bluff a Gospel Training Institute to prepare evangelists for this work. 2. "Scandalous" drinking in colleges was causing general anxiety. President Willard, recalling her own fun-loving youth, urged young women's leagues to provide wholesome sports. They must work out their problems of social decency in their own way. It was in one of these leagues that young Mary McDowell of Evanston began training for civic reform, a training continued at Hull House. 3. More important than either of these was education. From the first Miss Willard had argued that this would "yield the largest dividends." Hence the Union must engage specialists to train teachers in day and Sunday schools. It must find authors qualified to write temperance textbooks and interest publishers. It must gather children into Bands of Hope. To reach adults boxes of temperance literature must be placed in post offices and railway stations. There must be loan libraries of temperance books. Churches must be asked to use unfermented wine at communion.

All these projects the convention heartily endorsed. Mrs. Mary H. Hunt of Boston was elected to push the work of education, with men of distinction here and abroad as advisers. The writing of textbooks was authorized. Scientific investigation of the character and effects of alcoholic beverages was planned. States were offered aid in campaigning for a law requiring all schools supported by federal or state funds — including West Point and Annapolis — "to give a prescribed amount of instruction in the physiological effects of alcohol." Congress was asked to appoint a commission to investigate the cost and the results of the liquor traffic.

Other agenda of this first convention under new leadership included the demand for industrial and evening schools, and the promotion of better relations between capital and labor. Causes for rejoicing were new alliances: with the National Education Association and with summer assemblies. Chautauqua, Old Orchard Beach, Lake Bluff, Thousand Island Park and others had each set apart a W.C.T.U. day.

In 1880 the Union endorsed woman suffrage — the same Union that four years before had frowned upon an idea so radical and rebuked its champion; the same Union that two years before had debated hotly whether to seek suffrage for women even in local option. Elated, Miss Willard prophesied that before the end of that generation women would be voting in many states. Her prophecy was fulfilled; but women still had forty years to wait for suffrage in national affairs. And, contrary to her expectation, national prohibition would win first, without woman's vote. She had, however, guessed aright that there would be " a profound change in the convictions of the thoughtful and conscientious " and " a remolding of public sentiment such as this class always brings about when aroused."

In 1880 she reiterated her argument for a prohibition amendment (still as a loyal Republican): " We base our plea on the principle set forth by the Supreme Court of the country: 'No legislature can bargain away the public health or the public morals; the people themselves cannot do it, much less their servants. Government is organized with a view to their preservation, and cannot divest itself of the power to provide for them.' "

That public health and public morals were far from being fostered she quoted statistics to show: ten thousand murders in the United States during the year just past; six thousand suicides; twelve lynchings a month. And Judge Davis of New York, who had been twenty years on the bench, declared that ninety per cent of the crime was due to strong drink. "That which the people have legalized," Miss Willard averred, "they can render illegal."

She declared that high license was a "pitiably inadequate" measure, the worst of all schemes for controlling the liquor traffic, since those who vote for it "lose sight of the fact that they have legalized a traffic that will render necessary the expense of almshouse, hospital, insane asylum, and penitentiary." To her, high license was "moral chloroform."

She had now taken her stand squarely on three issues: *for* woman suffrage, *for* prohibition, and *against* high license. One day her Union would take its stand beside her on all three issues; but the time was not yet. She could wait. She would win "by evolution, not revolution."

No sooner, then, was she president of the National W.C.T.U. than she resolved to make the organization truly "national." In 1883, the Union would celebrate woman's first decade in temperance, reckoning the Hillsboro Crusade as the beginning. She resolved that by then there should be a union in every state and territory under the Stars and Stripes. It was a herculean labor. Since no one else offered, she would be the Hercules.

She had not forgotten that audience of nine thousand women in the Moody Tabernacle and the sense of power they had given her. Nine thousand women carrying into their homes the gospel of the great evangelist. So she must reach thousands of homes with the gospel of temperance. "Alone we can do little," she said; "aggregated we become batteries of power. . . . We want all those like-minded with us, who would put down the dramshop, exalt the home, . . . to join hands with us for organized work according to a plan." But dramshops would not be put down and the home exalted, she argued, so long as men's demand for liquor was met. Hence liquor must be denied them.

The East and the Midwest were already pretty well organized. Nothing had as yet been done in the South and the New West. So, early in 1881, accompanied by Anna Gordon and her sister Bessie and Mrs. McLean of Washington, Miss Willard went south. First, however, they called upon the newly inaugurated President Garfield to ask for his support, only to find that political success had made him cautious toward reforms. He whose campaign had promised them so much, now that he was in power had nothing to offer.

Disappointed but not disheartened, they turned then to the other part of their mission in Washington — the presentation to the White House of a life-size portrait of Lucy Webb Hayes, in recognition of her valiant teetotalism while First Lady. For, not content merely to turn down her own wineglass, Mrs. Hayes had permitted no liquor to be served, even at diplomatic dinners. David Huntington of New York, president of the National Academy of Design, had painted the portrait, and students of the Cincinnati Art School under the supervision of Ben Pittman had carved the frame. In her speech of presentation, Miss Willard paid tribute to the arts and their influence.

"There are," she said, "three mighty realms of influence which the temperance reform . . . has hardly yet invaded. The world of fine arts, of romance, and of fashion still sneers at total abstinence. From the days of Homer and Virgil to those of Tennyson and Longfellow, the poets have been singing the praises of wine. From Praxiteles to Powers, the sculptors have delighted to idealize the coarse features of Bacchus. From the antique frescoes of Pompeii down the choicest pigments of the painter have been lavished to furnish forth convivial feasts. . . .

The poet, the artist and the novelist, mighty interpreters of nature and the soil, will always maintain their empire over the human heart, so long as it is a willing captive to the love of beauty and the beauty of love. . . . Until we win a place for the temperance reform in these supremely influential realms of thought and expression, our success cannot be considered permanent."

From Washington the party set out for its tour of the South, sponsored by Mrs. Sallie F. Chapin of Charleston, South Carolina. Everywhere the northerners were cordially received. Everywhere Miss Willard was surprised at the honest effort being made to educate the Negroes, small though the appropriations had to be. Whites asked her to address meetings of Negroes; once a Negro spoke at a meeting of whites and former slaves. Tributes of gratitude were paid her and her work. One southern woman said, "It was the first ray of hope that had come into our lives since the war." Another "lay awake all night for sheer gladness . . . and took courage." Bishop Stevens, who as Colonel Stevens was said to have fired the first shot on Fort Sumter, suggested that "W.C.T.U." might stand for "We Come To Unite."

The tour was a decided success. Thenceforth large delegations of southern women came to W.C.T.U. conventions, and the South was well represented among the delegates assembled to celebrate the first decade.

Two years later, early in 1883, Miss Willard and Miss Gordon set out on what they called their "Temperance Roundup." This carried them thirty thousand miles, to every state and territory, to every capital but two (Arizona's and Idaho's), and to every town of ten thousand inhabitants or more, west of the Missouri. It was an extraordinary feat. Transportation was uncertain and often primitive, roads were poor or practically nonexistent. Few women could have borne the strain. But to these two resilient spirits pioneer travel, with its " unsuspected dangers," was full of " delightful surprises."

The tour was not without its thrills. Once, in the course of a three-day journey by " covered conveyance " across a hundred and eighty-two miles of prairie and mountain, they passed a spot where, several days previously, bandits had held up a stage, and again they were shown logs from behind which bandits had fired only the day before. But thrills were what Frances Willard needed to enliven her life of business routine. Doubtless she regretted not seeing a few bandits herself.

Her seemingly frail body was governed by an inflexible will, and constantly renewed by long hours of dreamless sleep. She gives as her daily program: " Up at seven or seven-thirty; all day reading and writing [letters]. Arrived at destination, a short rest; the evening lecture, followed by a cup of bread-and-milk or beef-tea. Soon asleep, usually for eight hours. No work after six o'clock except a lecture."

Tasks were adventures; hardships were novelties; the campaign never lacked the drama of suspense. For example, having journeyed eighty miles up Snake river by steamer, they reached Lewiston, only to hear that the mayor had that day prohibited all public meetings " through fear of an epidemic of diphtheria." Many residents thought it was " through fear of a temperance crusade." Nevertheless, the union was organized in a private house, and on the way back to the steamer friends, who filled the coach, served tea.

Since the National Union was as yet too poor to pay salaries — much less finance journeyings of such magnitude as these — the " roundup " would have been impossible had it not been for passes given by railway and steamship companies, a gift of three hundred dollars from the Good Templars of California, and the generous hospitality offered everywhere.

(X)

The W.C.T.U. and Politics

IN HIS *George Washington* RUPERT HUGHES STAMPS AS " POOR patriotism, ridiculous idolatry and rank dishonesty " failure to give due credit to all who carried their leader to victory. None felt this more keenly than Frances Willard; none was more generous in praise of those other strugglers. As she faced the convention of 1883, she must have thought with pride of the women — most of whom, including some from Evanston, were present — who had founded and established this great organization, women stout of heart and wise in counsel.

There was Mary A. Livermore, primarily a suffragist, but the only one of her friends to say to her in 1874, " Your place is in temperance." Often they had spoken from the same platform, or been denied a hearing because of their " radical " principles. With the Chicago delegation sat Louise S. Rounds, whose appeal had led the ex-dean to decline the security and comparative ease of a fashionable girls' school for insecurity and hardship in an obscure circle of Chicago reformers. In the Maine delegation was Mrs. L. M. N. Stevens, first met at Old Orchard Beach on that tour of inspection to determine what promise lay in the new temperance movement. Most intimate comrade during the decade had been J. Ellen Foster of Iowa, who had written the National Union's constitution. So at one were she and Miss Willard in ideas, and so ready to carry them through, that they were called the " wheel-horses " of the Union. On the platform sat Annie Wittenmeyer, crusader and the Union's first president. Michigan had sent Mary T. Lathrap ("with the brain of a man") and Mrs. S. M. I. Henry ("with the spirit of a saint"). From Ohio were "Mother" Stewart and Mrs. Thompson, crusaders *cum laude;* from Indiana, Zerelda Wallace, wife of the governor and stepmother of General Lew Wallace. Sallie F. Chapin led the delegation from the South.

Representing Illinois were Jennie F. Willing, first woman to be ordained by the Methodist Church, and Matilda B. Carse, founder of the Woman's Temperance Publication Association, who had dedicated herself to raising eight hundred thousand dollars to build a Woman's Temple, to house the National Union. With them were clear-headed Ruby Gilbert, Mrs. Carse's accountant; Esther Pugh, national treasurer; and Helen Hood ("Hoodie"), whose ability as state treasurer led to her later being retained for years as consultant by the British Women's Temperance Association.

The president's eye rested most lovingly, perhaps, on her old friends and neighbors in the Evanston delegation: Mrs. E. E. Marcy from across the street; Mary B. Willard, founder of the first W.C.T.U. free kindergarten in Evanston; Emily Huntington Miller, coeditor with Edward Eggleston of the *Little Corporal,* forerunner of the *St. Nicholas Magazine*. She, with Mrs. Willing and Mrs. Brown, had issued the call to the convention out of which had grown this thriving Union.

It had been a good decade, the president felt. But others had paved the way for them. She was not ignorant of the debt her Union owed the past. "Only those unread in the biography of genius," she said once, "imagine themselves to be original. . . . There is no reform which some great soul had not dreamed of centuries ago." In temperance there was Dr. Benjamin Rush, signer of the Declaration of Independence, who from his chair in the University of Pennsylvania made war on

" ardent spirits." There was Oglethorpe, soldier-philanthropist, who, having founded a carefully selected colony, excluded liquor, lest the fiber of the men he sought to rehabilitate be weakened. Congress itself in the early days of the republic had considered legislation to put an end to distilleries. Early Presidents viewed the problem with concern. In his youth John Adams had led a campaign against the liquor traffic. Washington attributed to drink " the ruin of half the workmen in the country." Jefferson said that, if he were to live his life over again, he would ask every candidate for office whether he used ardent spirits, so harassed was he by the befuddled brains of men entrusted with government.

There had been, too, earlier organizations than theirs to combat drunkenness: local groups following on the heels of the first temperance society at Moreau, New York, in 1808; then the American Temperance Society; then the aggressive movement growing out of Lyman Beecher's " Six Sermons on Intemperance " in 1826. In nine years eight thousand societies were formed, at a time when the total population of the United States — according to the census of 1830 — was less than thirteen millions.

Till then the war had been on " ardent spirits " only — whisky, brandy, gin, rum, and other distilled liquors. Little beer and wine were made in America. But with the ban on hard liquors, soft drinks — beer, wine and cider — became popular, and drunkenness did not abate. There seemed no alternative to following the lead of the Teetotal party in England. Teetotalism, therefore, became the goal. The Washingtonian movement set out to reform. The Sons of Temperance, more aggressive, for a time drove saloons out of business; distilleries ran half-time; local option made headway. But bootleggers multiplied. Little by little, teetotalers backslid.

By that time the temperance movement had reached a period Miss Willard could remember, when the Maine prohibition law was passed in 1851. One state after another followed Maine, till all New England was under prohibition. By 1856 thirteen states were "dry." Illinois was divided in opinion: in the northern counties, Lincoln was advocating prohibition and forecasting a time when there would be neither slave nor drunkard. In the southern counties, Douglas was as vigorously opposing prohibition. In those days, it is said, prohibition was more popular than abolition.

And then, for twenty-five years, there were no prohibition states added. On the contrary, in one state after another, the law was declared unconstitutional. Some states returned to high license; some permitted beer, cider and wine. In 1870, there remained but three prohibition states.

Now, in 1883, prohibition was again on the upgrade. Surveying the victories and defeats of the past, Frances Willard felt the cause still worth championing. Prohibition, with strict enforcement, was her goal.

As she looked out over that sea of faces, she must have marveled at what had been accomplished in ten years to stabilize women and fit them for leadership. The success of great suffragists had encouraged pleaders of other causes. She may have recalled the day when Susan B. Anthony had spoken at the woman's college of Northwestern as guest of the dean. Unobtrusive in dress as the fashion of the day would permit, quiet in manner, simple, straightforward and concise in argument, with a never failing dash of humor, she spoke like a lawyer pleading his case in the court of public opinion.

When the Woman's Christian Temperance Union was formed in 1874, few women could organize a speech; fewer still could speak without notes; still fewer could argue a case without being too sentimental. She herself, Miss Willard knew, was too sentimental at times. In 1874, women had known little about financing anything bigger than a "ladies' aid" or a missionary society. No national association of women approaching in size the growing W.C.T.U. had yet been conceived. Already the financial problems involved, the publications increasing by tens of thousands of pages a year, the complexities of organization, made the Union a business corporation demanding an increasing number of experts.

Far from being the heterogeneous mob of fanatics the press enjoyed ridiculing, the Union was, its president said, a compact, well-organized army, "a *great educational agency* for women," such as they could create to combat any evil that threatened society.

It was a notable convention, the W.C.T.U.'s celebration of its first decade. There was great rejoicing that the Union was really national. Local option was spreading. Kansas had joined the prohibition states; Iowa was preparing to follow. Vermont, New Hampshire and Michigan had adopted scientific temperance instruction. The white-ribboners had become persistent lobbyists, memorializing Congress for woman's ballot and National Committees for a plank favoring a referendum on national prohibition.

Through five departments or more the Union had combated intemperance with information on heredity and hygiene; it had established free kindergartens and kitchen gardens; it had secured in several states a law requiring scientific temperance instruction, and had prepared suitable textbooks. It had organized children into Bands of Hope, and had sought to stay the heavy drinking in colleges and universities by organizing young women. Its Flower Mission, in the hands of Jennie C. Cassidy, a helpless invalid, had brought comfort and cheer to shut-ins and inmates of hospitals, workhouses and jails. Miss Willard once compared the Union to a growing network of telegraph lines. "Slow, difficult and adventurous," said she, "is the work of building these lines, establishing the stations, enlisting and teaching the operators." Her constant injunction was, "Apply your intelligence, your common sense to the problem." Again the Union was to her a great missionary movement for what its members called gospel temperance.

Says Miss Gordon: "She saw that the army called into existence by the ravages of the saloon upon the home could, with proper leadership, be arrayed likewise against every other evil which threatens the home and strikes at our civilization. She saw a great educational agency for women, and this ideal gave strength and courage for the ceaseless journeyings, difficult and distant, which were to mark [this period] of her life."

Yet she had no illusions as to the impossibility of making headway without popular support. She said: "The keystone of law can be firm and secure only when held in place by the arch — public sentiment. The more you can enlist in favor of your law the natural instincts of those who have the power to make that law and to select the officers who shall enforce it, the more securely stands the law."

Proudly she declared, "The Woman's Christian Temperance Union was never weak; it is a giant now." While in her address she gave them credit for these achievements, those most closely associated with her realized how conscientiously she had tried to gauge her pace to the abilities of her followers. But she would not have been Frances Willard had she not sometimes obeyed the urge to take a stride too long for most of them. She must know more of the world and the part she was to play in it. She must brave encounters and follow unblazed trails, knowing not whether they would end on a mountaintop or on the brink of a chasm. It was only thus that her soul could grow.

We have run ahead of our story in order to complete the account of the Union's first decade, a period of well-defined and steady progress, undisturbed by discord. Some leaders might have been satisfied with that; not Frances Willard. With calm disregard of consequences, she had two years before (1881) taken the most daring step of her career. She had known it would cost her " much good will and many votes." Yet she had made her new conviction the first item in her annual address in the fall of 1882.

" When the National Prohibition party held its convention in Cleveland in 1880," she said, " women were invited to attend as delegates. But, while I admired the progressive spirit thus indicated, it seemed to me clearly my duty not to go. Always profoundly interested in politics as the mightiest force on earth except Christianity, and trained to be a staunch Republican, both my education and my sympathies were arrayed on Garfield's side. . . . In contrast to the apathy with which we regarded the third-party movement, was the enthusiasm that greeted General Garfield's name at our annual meeting . . . we hailed his election as an answered prayer." She needed not to remind them — though she did — of their later disillusionment.

Her tour of the South, she continued, had first awakened in her the hope of a party " along longitudinal lines," making for a " re-United States." But such a party could be neither Republican nor Democratic. Neither of these old parties could unite victor and vanquished of the Civil War. To each party she gave credit for much needed reforms in the past. But to her the old parties were has-beens. For on what she deemed the greatest issue pending — prohibition of the manufacture and sale of intoxicating liquors — the ranks of each were split. "The Republicans of Maine, New Hampshire and Vermont vote for it; the Republicans of North Carolina, Ohio and Illinois against it; the Democrats of Kansas oppose, and of South Carolina favor it! I blame neither party, [but] 'a house divided against itself cannot stand.'" Then, with that never failing glint of humor that turned aside wrath, she added, "This is saying nothing whatever against the house; it is recognizing the law of gravitation, that is all."

Many of the listeners knew that the year before their president had attended a meeting called to reorganize the Prohibition party, that she was now a member of the party's National Committee, and spoke publicly in the party's behalf. But they knew also that she had announced publicly that this was a personal allegiance and did not involve the W.C.T.U.

The Prohibition party was formed in Chicago in 1869. For twelve years Miss Willard ignored it. Old party ties were still strong. But in 1881, at the convention of the National Temperance Society, she had met the leaders of the party, and at once recognized their moral and intellectual worth. They were men who could supply the mental stimulation she needed. She and they could cooperate for social and political betterment. Temperance was not their only goal, nor was it hers.

Two months later she met them at another temperance convocation, this time at Lake Bluff, near Chicago. When a "reformed" man begged that they "stop talking and *do* something," she recalled that a cousin of hers, also "reformed," had said, "Cousin Frank, you people ought to go into politics. You'll never succeed till you do."

That night she could not sleep (though a famous sleeper) for thinking of those two men, asking for help to fight their battle against drink. What to do? Old means had failed. Before morning she had resolved that, for better, for worse, she would cast in her lot with these men and women who sought a new world by "doing something" at the polls. Her decision meant turning her back on the Republican party, which she still loved; it meant antagonizing many with whom she had hitherto been in hearty accord. "It meant," says Miss Gordon, "courage to be branded as a fanatic and an iconoclast." But, convinced that woman's ballot was essential to the preservation of the home, she set out to find how it might be secured through a party uncorrupted by professional politicians.

She saw in the Prohibitionists a party after her own heart, led by "political philosophers" whose theories of government harmonized with her own. Already she knew Neal Dow of Maine, who, as mayor of Portland, had in 1851 pushed the Maine prohibition law through the legislature and, what is more, *enforced it*. She knew by reputation Chief Justice Salmon P. Chase and General Benjamin F. Butler, the party's candidates for the presidential nomination. John B. Finch had been long active in temperance campaigns, and was soon to be Grand Chief Templar. Samuel Dickie was not only a good astronomer but a good logician and executive as well. John P. St. John, governor of Kansas, had been influential in pushing through (by referendum) the first prohibition amendment to a state constitution. Iowa was now looking to him for help in securing a similar amendment.

Miss Willard was most impressed by James Black of Pennsylvania and John Russell of Michigan. Black, a lawyer of brilliant intellect, had been originally a Democrat, but in 1856 had helped organize the Republican party and been a delegate to its first convention. He had been Grand Chief Templar, and had tried to secure passage of a Maine law in his own state.

Russell was credited with being the master builder of his party's program, for which he had long prepared the way through his *Peninsular Herald* of Detroit.

Since political parties, like everything else, must be financed, this one was happy to have at its disposal the coffers of Gerrit Smith, New York millionaire and dyed-in-the-wool reformer. In days when prohibition had been more popular than abolition, he had been twice presidential candidate of the Abolition party.

Miss Willard was quick to recognize the far-sighted statesmanship shown in the party's platforms. Looking back, we read with surprise that a party often regarded as insignificant, championed in the platform of 1872 four constitutional amendments which eventually became laws of the land, though not till long after those early champions had turned to dust: direct election of senators, prohibition, woman suffrage, and income tax. Other planks of that platform were civil service based on merit, sound money, and reforms in transportation that eventuated in the Interstate Commerce Commission fifteen years later.

In 1876, the platform had included planks still newer, such as international arbitration, suppression of gambling (including gambling in stocks and produce), abolition of barbarous punishments in jails and prisons, and crime prevention by prison reforms. Most radical of all, perhaps, was "reduction of salaries of public officers *in a just ratio with the decline of wages and market prices*"!

For years Miss Willard had been emphasizing the need of "grounding" prohibition in a constitutional amendment, "beyond the reach of demagogues." She had been pointing out the need of officers who would enforce the law — officers who could be secured only through a *party* that would create and operate the machinery for enforcement. Knowing human frailty, she tried to forestall criticism by urging that, even if prohibition did not always prohibit, neither did civilization always civilize, nor Christianity always Christianize.

In 1883, she could report that the Illinois W.C.T.U. had gone so far as to recommend that aid be given the third party "to put in nomination in each district a candidate committed to vote for the submission of a constitutional amendment giving the full ballot to the women of Illinois, as a means of protecting their homes"; and that straightway the Liquor League of Illinois had countered with instructions to fight every nominee who could not be "fully relied on to vote in favor of personal liberty." Again her smile, though this time with a barb in it, as she added, "They want protection, too!"

"There is still a party in the land," she pleaded, "to be helped onward to success by women. There is one now despised for the single reason that it lacks majorities and commands no high positions as the rewards of skillful leadership or wily caucusing, but which declares as its cardinal doctrine that a government is impotent indeed which cannot protect the lowliest home from the aggressions of the vilest saloon. . . . It declares all issues trifling when compared with this."

Her reasons, then, for helping the Prohibition party were three: that it gave promise of binding together North and South in a common cause; that it aimed to bring about federal prohibition of the liquor traffic; that its platform was based on a "political philosophy" which called for a broader democracy.

It was done! In championing that party she had committed the unpardonable sin. Dearly as she loved her throne, she had challenged fate to dethrone her. The convention felt the tensity of the crisis when she ended quietly but dramatically with Luther's challenge to the Diet of Worms: "Here I stand; I can do no other. God help me! Amen."

Was it "amen" to her career in the Union she loved? It

was one thing for women to ask old parties to fight for prohibition; but to forswear the old parties to which they had given fealty, the parties of their men folk, and ally themselves with a party as yet untried, was quite a different thing. The proposal met with strong opposition, led by Mrs. J. Ellen Foster, hitherto the president's staunch supporter.

Strong as the opposition was, it did not cost her a throne. The convention took no official action. It loved its leader, often as she strayed from the strait and narrow way of temperance only. Ardent Prohibitionist though she was, her followers recognized her reliance on public opinion.

Dr. D. Leigh Colvin quotes her as saying: "We have the tariff to protect industry, patent laws for the inventor, subsidies for steamship companies, land grants for railways, charters for corporations, but for the homes of America we have no adequate protection from the dramshops."

(XI)

Battles and Bright Interludes

IN 1884 FRANCES WILLARD TOOK PART FOR THE FIRST TIME IN a presidential campaign, as W.C.T.U. delegate to the Committee on Resolutions of each party. Her Union was asking for a plank favoring a prohibition amendment to the Constitution. She went first to the Greenback convention and, seated in a box beside Mrs. Zerelda Wallace, heard her memorial presented in a fine speech and loudly applauded. Applause, however, was all she got from that party.

Next she visited the Republican committee, which at the request of Senator Blair grudgingly granted her fifteen minutes in which to present her case. Watch in hand, she spoke thirteen minutes and withdrew. But, though Kansas, Iowa and Maine were represented on the committee, it unanimously adopted a platform without a temperance plank. " So, then and there," she says, " I bade the ' Grand Old Party ' an everlasting farewell, and took my line of march toward the Grand Army of Reform." But not till she had been cold-shouldered by the Democratic committee.

That ordeal over, she gladly turned her steps toward Pittsburgh, where the Prohibitionists were meeting. Prolonged cheers on her entrance left no room for doubt that here, at least, she was welcome. The gaily decorated hall, the seven hundred delegates (not politicians but the sort of folks she was accustomed to), made her feel at home, a feeling she never lost in what she called " the greatest party."

At the request of the Kansas delegation, she seconded the

nomination of Governor St. John for president, and afterward she spoke also at the ratification meeting at Cumberland, Maryland. She threw herself with the zeal of an apostle into the campaign for two things she believed would some day usher in the " Republic of God " — woman suffrage and prohibition.

After her death fourteen years later, an editor paid her this tribute: " The *Outlook* has differed radically with her on two important points. We do not believe in prohibition by the state, and she has been its most eloquent advocate; we do not believe in woman suffrage, and she has done more to overcome woman's instinctive aversion to the ballot than any other representative of that cause."

An influential factor in the Prohibition campaign of 1884 was *Voice,* published by Funk and Wagnalls as the party organ, and long an effective advocate. It supported the leadership of what it called " men of intelligence," and made its appeal to men and women who thought. And so successful was this appeal that in the next four years (1884–88) more than one Republican paper, says Dr. Colvin, sounded a note of warning to its party, while the Prohibition vote increased seventy per cent.

In 1884 Prohibitionists were proud of the quality of their nominees for governor in many states: in Massachusetts, President Seelye of Amherst; in Illinois, J. B. Hobbs, former president of the Chicago board of trade; in Wisconsin, S. D. Hastings, four times state treasurer; in Michigan, David Preston, Detroit banker.

The outcome of the election was that Blaine of the " golden tongue," six years Speaker of the House, was defeated; Cleveland, scarcely known outside his own state, was victorious. The balance had hung on the electoral role of New York state, says Dr. Colvin, where the Prohibitionists had polled 24,999 votes.

But Woodrow Wilson ascribes the Democratic victory not to the Prohibitionists (whom he does not even mention in his *History of the American People*), but to the "mugwumps" of New York—"Republicans," says he, "who repudiated Blaine for a young man who, as mayor and governor in his own state, had proved his quality." He suggests that it had not helped Blaine that he had written Garfield four years before warning him against reformers as "the worst possible political advisers . . . foolish, vain, without knowledge of measures, ignorant of men." But that was not all. In Blaine's eyes, the reformers were pharisaical, ambitious, pretentious. But Cleveland, says Wilson, knew "the sterling character and wide experience of the particular group of reformers who had made his election possible." Though Blaine referred specifically to the mugwumps, other reformers resented his epithets none the less. Such of them as had voted the Prohibition ticket had no regrets when Blaine lost the presidency.

The W.C.T.U. shared in the hostilities following the election when Prohibitionists and Greenbackers were held responsible for the Republican defeat, though together they had cast but three hundred fifty thousand votes out of ten million. Prohibitionists were shunned; Prohibition preachers lost their pulpits. John P. St. John was hanged in effigy, and lost the renomination for governor of Kansas. St. John county, Kansas, was renamed. "We did not appreciate the anger of a party in defeat," said Miss Willard in convention. "Indeed, we had not supposed that defeat was in store for the Republicans."

The chief value of the campaign, perhaps, was in warning old parties to change their attitude toward temperance reform. Thereafter they showed more willingness to enact laws for scientific education in temperance, and by 1901 every state had adopted such a law. Even Congress passed such a law for the

District of Columbia. For eight years Congressman Henry W. Blair (later Senator Blair) had been introducing in Congress a resolution for a constitutional amendment prohibiting the manufacture and sale, first of distilled liquors, then of all alcoholic liquors. Though the resolution died in committee year after year, it served to keep the subject alive.

Frances Willard said philosophically, "If this work be of God, it cannot be overthrown; if it be not, then the sooner it comes to naught, the better for humanity."

When, after the election, the W.C.T.U. came under the ban of the Republican party, Miss Willard sent this message to the locals: "To be tolerant is a difficult grace; yet its exercise is imperiously demanded of us. A party long accustomed to succeed is in defeat. Thousands of leading men see their hopes blighted, ambitions overthrown, perhaps their occupations gone. Party journals denounce the Prohibitionists as having caused all this. . . . The W.C.T.U. is termed a 'political party' and subjected to the sharpest criticism by men who found no fault with our societies in Iowa, Kansas, and other states where they 'lent their influence' to the Republicans." She ended with a reminder of "him who, when he was reviled, reviled not again, but committed himself to him who judgeth righteously."

This was no preachment or pious pose, but a bit of encouragement to those who were likely to fall by the wayside. She said in effect: Let us be careful not to do a similar injustice; let us realize that they, too, are sincere. We seek the same goal, but have chosen different roads.

Even before the election the Union was made to feel the repercussions of its president's hobnobbing with the unpopular party. For the first time it found itself unwelcome in the city where its convention was scheduled to meet. St. Louis churches were closed to it; homes once hospitable no longer offered entertainment to delegates. When the prospect seemed darkest, Reverend John A. Wilson, of the United Presbyterian Church, who had traveled with Miss Willard in the Holy Land, persuaded his church to admit the outcasts.

For her annual address the president had chosen the timely theme "Gospel Politics." After congratulation on the achievements of the year, she launched into what was now her constant topic: "In the field of national prohibition we shall fight our hardest battles and win our most substantial victories." For fifty years, she said, men and women had been trying to create public sentiment against the liquor traffic. They had failed because their efforts were sporadic. What the temperance reform needed most was unification of effort, concentration upon the enactment of a national constitutional amendment.

But the convention would go no farther than to reaffirm its intention to lend its influence to *any party* with a prohibition plank in its platform. Not till 1887 did the annual debate come to an end. Then, tired of the useless wrangle with a steadily diminishing minority, the convention decided that "any resolution referring to our attitude toward political parties be decided *without discussion*." Frances Willard had won, and a large majority of her Union were with her.

The heat of battle cooled. In 1885 forty churches in Philadelphia, its convention city, were offered the Union. It chose, however, to meet in Association Hall, which it gaily decorated with state and local escutcheons. This was the Union's largest convention to date, with two hundred and eighty-two delegates from forty states and territories. The hostilities of the previous year had not "set the temperance movement back twenty years," as some had predicted. This was a record-breaking convention, at which work was laid out for forty-four departments, radiating into all walks of life. " A scientific age," said the president, " requires the study of every subject in all its correlations. Every question of practical philanthropy has its temperance aspect, and with that we are to deal."

No one was surprised, therefore, when the Union initiated another new department, designed to promote social purity, with an equal standard for men and women. It took the name White Cross, immediately suggestive of another rescue band, the Red Cross. Twelve years of temperance work had taught them, said Miss Willard, that the saloon and the brothel were Siamese twins.

Nearly twenty years before, in Paris, she had often seen closed black-covered wagons passing along the street. On inquiry she had learned that, while Paris issued permits for houses of ill fame, it limited the hours when and the streets where prostitutes might walk. It required, too, that once a week they go, under police escort, to the dispensary for physical examination, to guard against communicable disease. To one who till then had spent most of her life in the country or in villages, or in the seclusion of college walls, the idea seemed horrible; it took prostitution for granted, as something to be tolerated rather than eradicated. Now, twenty years later, she insisted that the " let-alone " policy must cease. No vice could be tolerated in men that degraded women; here, as in everything else, there must be sex equality. What was wrong for women was equally wrong for men.

This conviction was not new. For years the Union had been endeavoring to reinstate " fallen " women in society. As early as 1879, Iowa women had founded a home for them. Maine had an Industrial Home in which they found shelter; New York, a Home for Inebriate Women; Cleveland, the Open Door; Chicago, the Anchorage. Many states had installed police matrons. A recent article, however, in the London *Pall Mall Gazette* had revealed the appalling extent of the social evil in England. Aroused by this call to decency, American women under the W.C.T.U. were following the lead of the Bishop of Durham, who had founded the British White Cross League, pledged to equal chastity for men and women. No longer was the "double standard" to obtain.

Soon another W.C.T.U. petition was in circulation. This time Congress was asked to impose heavier penalties for assault, and to raise the age of consent to eighteen. In Massachusetts and Vermont, said Miss Willard, it was a greater crime to steal a cow than to ruin a woman, while in Illinois seduction was not recognized as a crime. Congress compromised by raising the age of consent to sixteen years.

To head this new department, the Union sought a woman of "delicacy and ability." Three years later it found such a leader in Mrs. Laura Ormiston Chant, long acquainted with this work in England. "No department," says the president, "ever developed so rapidly." Industrial homes were founded by the states at the Union's request; efforts were made to segregate those physically and mentally unfit, and to place the "incapable" in institutions.

Thus twelve years after the birth of the movement to save fallen men the Union was just as earnestly at work to save fallen women. Temperance was not, indeed, Miss Willard's only goal. Lady Henry Somerset, one of her closest friends, calls the temperance cause only "the open door through which she entered into her service for the world." And she explains what many have forgotten, that in the defense of women — her main task — Frances Willard belonged "*to no special cause*."

Dr. C. J. Little of Evanston wrote in the *Chautauquan* in her defense: "Miss Willard has been criticized severely for blending with the cause of temperance the cause of woman suffrage and of social reform. From her point of view this was logical and inevitable. Her intellect was too strong and too sagacious not to perceive that temperance was, after all, not the main question. The main question was that of the home. . . . This involved the lifting of women to another plane, the plane of political equality with men. It involved also the lifting of the masculine standard of morality."

James Truslow Adams was thinking along similar lines when he saw that the question " splitting " America was not solely prohibition; that that involved " questions of social welfare, of economics, of entrenched interests, of class distinction in legislation, of personal liberty."

Most of Miss Willard's time was now given to conventions and lecturing. Many have paid tribute to her eloquence. Dr. Frank W. Gunsaulus recalled at her death the " harmonious swell of her voice, its flexibility and richness." He told of Wendell Phillips' astonishment at her repose and consciousness of power. Having recently got himself into hot water by a speech full of biting sarcasm, Phillips marveled at her restraint, and exclaimed, " It takes a woman to do that! " Dr. Frank M. Bristol ascribed her power to her " unfailing optimism, faith in God and justice, in humanity and right, feeling in her heart the prophecy of victory."

She had never forgotten Parker Earle's " appeal to intelligence, quoting statistics." Gamaliel Bradford refers again and again to her charm enhanced by infinite tact which stirred thousands, " made them anxious to carry out her ideas . . . whispered some spell of conviction."

Like others of her day, she made free use of figures of speech: " The two guardian angels of humanity are science and faith."

Woman's ballot is "that powerful sunglass [which] can be made to converge on the rumshop," and burn out "this cancerous excrescence." — "The whisky power looms like a Chimborazo among the mountains of difficulty over which we must climb to the land of our dreams." — "Vice is the tiger with keen eyes, alert ears, and catlike tread; virtue is the slow-paced, complacent elephant, whose greatest danger lies in its ponderous weight and consciousness of power." Then there are all those metaphors of warfare in a war-conscious age, such as, "Vice delights in keen-edged weapons; virtue's guns are unwieldy and slow to swing into range."

She was in constant demand as a speaker. What, then, came of that "spell of conviction," that "desire to carry out her ideas"? Bradford saw countless men and women living useful lives, filling positions of trust and responsibility, because she had stirred them to action and given them faith in themselves.

Bradford is just such an honest, nonpartisan champion as Frances Willard needs in an age that knows her not, nor understands what should be credited to her and what should not. To him she appears a woman of noble character, neither martyr nor saint, but one who never lost the zest of life.

Young Frank Willard, Miss Willard's erratic namesake, who concealed his identity in his pen name "Josiah Flynt" (his upright grandfather's, barring the substitution of *y* for *i*) gives us a look into the Willard home in these days: "When my aunt was at home, Rest Cottage was a regular beehive of industry. Secretaries and type-writers were at work from morning till night, while my aunt caught up with her voluminous correspondence [one says it was thirty thousand letters a year] in her famous Den. . . . To live in a celebrity's home we children did not appreciate. It was a mecca for reformers of all shades and grades from all over the world, and we grew up in the atmosphere of strong personalities . . . the village was proud to have such a distinguished daughter.

"The only male being living at Rest Cottage . . . there was a feminine atmosphere about things that used to get on my nerves. My aunt and I did not always get on well together. . . . When criticizing my escapades and backslidings, I have been told she was wont to say, 'Josiah has character and will power, but he wills to do the wrong things.'"

And so many, like poor Josiah, while they knew the right thing, willed to do the wrong, and go to the dogs.

After stumping the country for St. John in what was really an educational campaign; after riding the wave of bitter recrimination that followed Republican defeat; after organizing the White Cross and planning the world's W.C.T.U., Miss Willard went home to rest. One day there arrived at Rest Cottage a new-fangled thing called a tricycle. It was for her niece Katharine, now a young lady. From a window she watched Katharine, then Anna, circle the huge flower bed in the center of the back yard, and thought, "How easy!" Soon the two were taking turns spinning down the shady street in front of the house. Like "a war-horse sniffing the battle," she longed to get into action. She did. Having circled the flower bed, she must circle the block, and that in record-breaking time. The others had done it in two minutes and a half; she did it in two minutes and a quarter. "Not contented with this," she says, "but puffed up with foolish vanity, I declared that I would go around in two minutes."

The next she knew, she was crumpled up in the ditch, and realized that, for the first time in her life, she was badly hurt. She saw "Anna Gordon's white face, a stricken mother . . . two physicians, and a gas mask: then all sorts of foolish visions

— then heavenly peace." Her arm was set. But what weary weeks of sitting around doing nothing! Once she had said, "The chief wonder of my life is that I dare to have so good a time — physically, mentally and spiritually." This time, however, she had to pay dearly for her fun.

But that ether! Sometimes she wished she might take it again, "just for the ethical and spiritual help that came to me. It let me out into a new world, greater, more mellow, more godlike."

Perhaps it was that unfortunate ride that prompted the resolution on dress reform at the next convention. Says Miss Willard: "The versatility of the W.C.T.U. can hardly be better illustrated than by the fact that this same convention not only swung us into politics, but adopted a petition to editors of fashion-plate magazines," protesting "constriction of the waist and compression of the trunk . . . which deforms the body . . . results in injury to important vital organs . . . and an artificial standard of symmetry and beauty, through the influence of popular fashion plates."

Madam Willard's eightieth birthday, January 3, 1885, was the greatest holiday that Rest Cottage had ever seen. For it Frank and her sister-in-law, Mary B., issued twenty-five hundred invitations. The latter had returned from Berlin, where for several years she maintained a school for American students. With her had come her two daughters. Oliver's two sons were absent. Yet "Josiah" (who loved few, though himself so lovable) honored "this grandmother of mine" next to the mother he adored — adored, while he broke her heart. For it the busy secretaries and typists cleared away all evidence of work, and the Den was slicked up for visitors to see.

Frank and Mary B. twined into an arch the branches of the evergreens Mr. Willard had planted before the house-door.

"Reformed" men and their families hung grounds and arch with lanterns. Churchville, Oberlin and Forest Home sent evergreens and vines to decorate the house, where an anchor of flowers typified faith and a crown of flowers foretold the reward of the faithful. Gifts came from everywhere in the world until they filled the rooms.

On the evening of the great day relatives and intimate friends sat down to an early supper, followed by prayer and a hymn written for the occasion by Anna Gordon (too ill to be present). Then Evanston children came in a body to present eighty rosebuds — "because you are so sweet, grandma." Oliver's wife read from an album in which she had mounted them some of the greetings from afar: from Whittier, Neal Dow, John B. Gough, former President and Mrs. Hayes, Mr. and Mrs. Moody, Maria Mitchell, Roswell Smith of the *Century,* bishops, judges, and others. Mrs. Morton D. Hull recalled Madam Willard's ten years as president of the Evanston Union. Chicago's Union had embossed in vellum and handsomely framed its expression of appreciation of Frances Willard's enlistment with it little more than ten years ago.

From eight till eleven o'clock Madam Willard, seated in the fashionable Boston rocker Frank had just given her, and surrounded by portraits of her loved ones who had "gone over the river," received old Evanston friends and friends of Frank's she knew only by name. When the fit time came, she made a little speech of thanks, speaking slowly and with some difficulty, for the years, long and rather lonely, had taken their toll. "I appreciate your kindness and the honor you do me," she said. "But I am aware it is to an ideal you show this loving courtesy and unfeigned respect. . . . It does no harm when our friends put an overestimate upon us; it stimulates us to endeavor to be

Willard Hall, Evanston, Illinois

Northwestern Female College

Frances Willard and Anna Gordon

such persons as our friends charitably think we are. . . . I have a prayer in my heart for you all."

She had seven more years in which to give inspiration and caution to the daughter of whom she was both proud and vigilant. Seven years, passed mostly alone with the faithful Hannah — "glorying," says "Josiah," "in her daughter's fame and usefulness, and carefully pasting press notices of her work in a scrapbook." Shelves full of these scrapbooks still testify to her diligence.

"Pray for me, mother," Frank would say on leaving home.

"I do little but pray for you," her mother would answer.

It was for that her life was prolonged. It was because of her that Miss Willard could say with assurance, "Mother-love works magic, but organized mother-love works miracles."

(XII)

A World Union

WHILE IN CALIFORNIA IN 1883, MISS WILLARD RECEIVED MANY invitations to visit the Sandwich Islands (now the Hawaiian Islands), China and Japan. Much as she would have delighted in such a trip, it was not her place to go. But after witnessing in Chinatown the havoc wrought by linking opium with alcohol — "Occident and Orient combining to degrade" — she proposed at the next convention a commission to formulate plans for a World's W.C.T.U. Without waiting for the commission's report, she saw to it that Mrs. Mary Clement Leavitt was sent at once to the Sandwich Islands. From there, Mrs. Leavitt went to Australia, Japan, China, India, and across to Africa, undaunted by the tremendous obstacles to travel.

For seven years she journeyed thus, pinning the white ribbon on converts of every hue. Meanwhile a fund was created to carry on this work of world organization. One by one others followed Mrs. Leavitt, till there were five world organizers in the field. Whether in Europe, Asia, Africa, or South America, they found missionaries ready to aid them. Theirs is a thrilling story, but this is not the place for it. Suffice it to say that at Antwerp in 1885, on motion of Frances Willard, the British reformer Margaret Bright Lucas, sister of the statesman John Bright, was elected first president of the World's W.C.T.U. Later Miss Willard succeeded her, in what proved to be another life office.

The Union's motto was now changed from "For God and Home and Native Land" to "For God and Home and Every

Land." Within six years, the Union spread through fifty countries. It was "a world republic of women," said its president, "without distinction of race or color, who recognize no sectarianism in religon, no sex in citizenship. . . . Whatever touches humanity touches us."

To aid white-ribbon missionaries Miss Willard wrote her Polyglot Petition to the rulers of the world, asking for prohibition of traffic in opium and liquors. It was to be translated into every tongue and circulated for signatures. She argued that merely to organize, pin on badges, and pray with women the world over was not enough. They must be given something to do; they must feel they were cooperating with women in other lands. Such action in unison would make for international good will. In 1885, this petition was first presented by Mrs. Mary B. Willard at Antwerp.

In 1891, the World's W.C.T.U. held its first convention — in Faneuil Hall, Boston; in 1893, its second, in Chicago; in 1895, its third, in London; and in 1897 (the year before Miss Willard's death), its fourth, in Toronto.

Distinguished guests now came every year from other lands to attend the National Union's conventions. One who made a deep impression on all who heard her was Pundita Ramabai, who appealed to the Union, as "the largest-hearted band of women on earth," to do something for India's widows, especially the three-fifths who, being high-caste, could not be reached by missionaries. They could not marry again; but, if Christianized and trained in vocations, they might become the remolders of Hindu society. The pundita asked that American women form circles to lend support to her projected college for Hindu women.

Here was a woman of quite a new type. A Brahmin, she could trace her ancestry of teetotalers and vegetarians back a thousand years. Yet she had dared to break with the past by marrying out of her caste and sharing her husband's life as his equal. Her culture, intelligence and sincerity had won the cooperation of the British government in establishing elementary and, later, high schools for Indian girls, and in urging Hindu women to fit themselves for teaching and the practice of medicine.

Brahmin women, who had at first been shocked at her unconventionality, had now come to trust her, and societies to promote the education of girls were being formed in the larger cities of India. Through the influence of Max Müller she had been made professor of Sanskrit in Cheltenham College, England. It was from there she had come to America to attend the graduation in medicine of a high-caste Hindu woman.

Since Frances Willard was thenceforth to have the pundita's picture on her desk as one of four women so favored, we might look at the visitor through the eyes of her admirer: "A young woman of medium height, and ninety-eight pounds weight . . . lithe, quick, graceful . . . in simple dress of grayish silk and white chuddar — the white wrap of the East. . . . Gentle, quick of apprehension, adroit, equipoised, her wit sparkles in repartee." One can see what bound together these two women living on opposite sides of the world.

Frances Willard's interest in the "workers," though intensified now by the successes of the Knights of Labor, was nothing new. At Forest Home the "help" had been treated with the same consideration as the family. Those who could not read and write English had been taught, and every effort had been put forth to make them good citizens. They had gathered with the family for prayers — save Bridget, who declined to come in but listened from her seat on the other side of the door. Some had stayed till they married and set up homes of their own — Mike, for instance, who had given the girls their only pin money when they left for Milwaukee. Then there was Bertha, who had "got into trouble." They could not turn her out. They forced her betrayer to leave town; she and her baby remained in the Willard home.

A servant had once said to Frank: "I wonder if you ever think what a poor life it is for us who must be always managing to get a bit to eat and something to wear? We must be always working for the body and doing nothing for the soul. And yet after a while the body'll go away from us, but the soul you know never goes away."

It was with genuine feeling (and when wasn't she genuine?) that Miss Willard wrote: "While we sleep, a thousand hands are busy for us, gathering materials for our morning meal, passing on our letters by the swift train, printing our mental breakfast on the broad pages of the daily press. A thousand hands are moving that we may have cloth for our new suit, rapid transit when we leave home, books . . . music . . . inventors . . . philosophers. Some day the great world-mind, tutored and taught, will lend its mighty force to each child of humanity."

Therefore those who knew her best were not surprised when, at the Minneapolis convention in 1886, she asked permission to distribute an address to the Knights of Labor and other labor bodies.

The Knights of Labor had been founded in 1869, to secure better working conditions for both men and women. The organization's name suggested the dignity of labor and a fine idealism. By 1888 it had reached its peak and become international. But it was facing a new labor organization — one less idealistic and more aggressive — which would ultimately absorb it.

To these modern knights, then, this address went out: "To

all working Men and Women — Brothers and Sisters of a Common Hope: We come to you naturally as our friends and allies. With such of your methods as involve cooperation, arbitration, and the ballot box we are in hearty sympathy. Measures which involve compulsion of labor, the destruction of property, or harm to life or limb we profoundly deplore, and we believe the thoughtful and responsible among your ranks must equally deplore them, as not only base in themselves, but as a great hindrance to your own welfare and success. We rejoice in your broad platform . . . which recognizes neither sex, race, nor creed. Especially do we appreciate the tendency of your great movement to elevate women industrially . . . by claiming for them equal pay for equal work; recognizing them as officers . . . and advocating the ballot in their hands as their rightful weapon of self-help in our representative government.

"As temperance women, we have been especially glad to note your hostile attitude toward the saloon . . . the vow made by the newly elected officers . . . when, with hands raised to heaven, they pledged themselves to total abstinence. . . .

"The central question of labor reform is not so much *how to get more wages* as *how to turn present wages to better account.* . . . Fourteen hundred millions annually drawn, chiefly from the pockets of the workingman, by saloonkeepers and cigar dealers, means less flour in the barrel, less coal in the cellar, and less clothing for the laborers' families. . . . We suggest that, if by your request, pay day were universally changed from Saturday to Monday, this would do much to increase the capital at home."

After quoting insurance statistics to show that the life of the total abstainer was nearly twice that of the moderate drinker, Miss Willard passed to the field of education: "Half the children of the United States are being taught [by state law] the evil effects of intoxicating liquors upon the tissues of the body and the temper of the mind." She asked cooperation in securing laws for instruction in diet, dress, sleep, exercise and ventilation. She called attention to the White Cross pledge of equal chastity for men and women. She urged closing saloons on Sunday, and promised the aid of the Union in securing a Saturday half-holiday for workers. The address ended with a plea for their votes for prohibition and their prayers for the coming of brotherhood upon the earth.

The Knights were doubtless surprised at the number of W.C.T.U. activities called to their attention: work among railroad employees, lumbermen, herdsmen, miners, soldiers and sailors; free kindergartens, kitchen gardens, free libraries and reading-rooms, lodging houses and restaurants; rescue work for women and men. The Woman's Temperance Publishing House, they were told, had distributed in a year thirty million pages of literature, all set by women compositors. The *Union Signal* always had a good word for all lawful activities to better the lot of the workers.

Miss Willard did not at this time know Terence Vincent Powderly, fourteen years Master Workman of the Knights of Labor. Three times Powderly was elected mayor of Scranton, Pennsylvania; once he was commissioner general of immigration. Admitted to the bar in 1894 and to the United States Supreme Court in 1901, he became a recognized authority on problems of immigration at home and abroad.

A man of such quality inevitably became a power in Miss Willard's life after they met during the circulation of the petition for the protection of women and girls. Accompanied by Mrs. Hannah Whitall Smith, Miss Willard went to see Mr. Powderly, in the hope of interesting him in the White Cross. Fortunately Mrs. Rodgers, editor of the Knights' Journal, was a white-ribboner. Through her influence, the labor leader received them promptly, having been promised the conference would be brief.

Miss Willard pictures the "great" Powderly as a man of more than medium height, broad-shouldered but not robust, with clearcut profile, a magisterial nose and a military moustache. His eyes behind glasses looked weary but kindly.

Briefly she stated her errand. He took the petition, glanced it over, and excused himself to consult his "brothers." Shortly he returned. "If you will send me ninety-two thousand copies," he said, "they shall go to every local assembly of the Knights of Labor without expense to you, and with the recommendation that they be signed, circulated, and returned to you at Evanston."

With an exchange of courtesies, they parted; that was all. Soon after, his picture appeared on her desk with those of four women she had singled out: Elizabeth Fry, Josephine Butler, Frances Folsom Cleveland, and Pundita Ramabai. Powderly represented her ideal of manhood: he was a total abstainer and permitted no smoking in his presence; he worked unremittingly to make this a better world for workers. His organization was merged with the American Federation of Labor, but he continued to wield great influence.

The Knights declined, the Temperance Union grew in power. But to the last the two organizations cooperated to advance education, temperance, woman suffrage and arbitration.

Writing her autobiography in 1889, Miss Willard characterizes the year just past as, up to date, the most remarkable in the history of temperance reform. It was the year of a presidential election, and there was small hope that the politicians would devise any temperance legislation. But as it turned out, much was forced upon them that advanced woman's participation in politics. Since 1882, the Prohibition party had demonstrated the value of women helpers. Now the Republican party had organized a Woman's National Committee, with Mrs. J. Ellen Foster at its head. Republican women introduced speakers and spoke themselves; they paraded; they swelled the applause at rallies. Democratic women wore the red rose badge and waved handkerchiefs instead of clapping. But in neither party did women sit in council with men, as Miss Willard felt they should do. On the other hand, when the Prohibition convention met in Indianapolis, May 30, 1888, of the one thousand delegates about a hundred were women.

Never was a Prohibition convention more enthusiastic. It seated three colored delegates, and adopted a resolution demanding recognition of the rights of the colored race. It "rapturously cheered" the resolution on equal pay for equal work. It passed the prohibition plank solemnly by a rising vote. But woman's ballot, which had been included in the platform for sixteen years, found unexpected objectors. Even Neal Dow argued that this was not the time to add to the controversial question of prohibition the still more controversial one of woman suffrage. "Wait," said he, "till we have secured prohibition; then we will reward our faithful allies."

The proposed plank had, as usual, been written by Miss Willard. It differed from her former planks only by the addition of the assertion that suffrage "rests on no mere accident of race, color, sex, or nationality," and in demanding that "where withheld for any reason it be restored *on such an educational basis as the several state legislatures deem wise*." Two hours of hot debate followed.

Her plank was adopted by an overwhelming majority, and to her was accorded credit for the victory. For in the debate she had reminded General Dow that, though Maine had had prohibition for forty years, it had recently again denied to women the right to vote.

After the adoption of the resolution she received an "ovation." Men's hands stretched toward her; men's voices said, "You ought to be a happy woman." One said, "I wish your old mother had seen this!" When she asked one and another why he had voted for the plank, the answers were all tributes to home influence: "Oh, I was born a suffragist." "Women must help us save the nation, if it is ever saved." "My wife educated me." "I don't forget that my mother is a woman."

She walked in silence to her stopping-place, accompanied, she says, by the ghosts of the ten long years during which she had been battling for the right of women to vote. The first ghost was that of the year-old Union in 1875, when she had proposed that, since woman suffered most from the "rum curse," she be given power to close the dramshop door. The presiding officer had asked with manifest disapproval, "What will you do with this woman suffrage resolution?" And the treasurer had answered firmly, "I move we lay it on the table." No second. Then another voice, "I move it be accepted."

That lone champion had given the Chicago radical courage to continue to plead her cause — in what seemed to her broken words, but eloquent enough to pass the suffrage resolution. But the fight had not ended there. Every year it had been renewed, often against great odds. Today's reaffirmation by the Prohibition party was a heartening assurance of ultimate success.

The convention had opened on Decoration day, and Chairman Dickie asked Miss Willard to give the address of welcome to the "Army of the Blue and the Gray." Taking as her theme "The Greatest Party," she gave these delegates from the North and the South a heart-warming talk calculated to allay old animosities. First came party aims: nationalism as against sectionalism; aspirations of the wage-worker as against monopolies; the future in politics as against the past; the home vote with an educational test as against the saloon vote; prohibition of sin as against an alliance between sin and government. "Party machinery and the ambition of party leaders today stand between the people and their opportunity," she said. "We would clear the track for prohibition. We are bound to do it."

She closed with a story of 1863, when the opposing armies were encamped on opposite sides of the Rappahannock. On each side, bands were playing the sectional favorites. All at once, a single soldier started a song that knew nor North nor South. Company after company took it up. It crossed the river. And soon both armies were singing "Home, Sweet Home."

A fit ending for such a day. To Frances Willard it was something more. In all her thinking, in all her planning, home was the center of the universe. Whatever the issue, she was committed to what she believed would protect the home.

The wearing of a flower as a political badge had been introduced by the Primrose League of England. American Democrats had followed suit with a red rose. Not to be outdone, Miss Willard proposed a white rose for the Prohibitionists, to match the white ribbon of the W.C.T.U. It was adopted.

So ended the second and last Prohibition convention in which Frances Willard took part. Four years later, she was in England; eight years later, the Prohibition party was split on the question of free silver; twelve years later, her work on earth had ended. After her death, the W.C.T.U. became nonpartisan.

By this time woman suffrage was a live issue at each party convention. But even the Chicago *Tribune* (Republican) made editorial protest against the discourtesy shown women of the

" suffrage sect " by the Republican National Committee after a woman had been granted the floor. Its members set up " cries of derision," heedless of the chairman's gavel. " The entire body of men became a howling mob . . . they shrieked, yelled, shouted, laughed, rushed about caucusing. . . . The suffrage delegate kept the platform undaunted. Not a word she uttered after the first twenty was heard."

The editor, however, agreed with his party in feeling that the suffragists, " especially those identified with the *twin fad* of prohibition," only played into the hands of the Democrats. But to him, as he revealed next day in discussing the " basis of woman suffrage," " all government was a matter of coercion or compulsory obedience." The real government of a community, he said, was represented by its police, militia, army and navy. The ballot was given to the fighting element. Woman was sexually disqualified for these services, hence for the suffrage.

It was an old argument. Miss Willard replied, " They say we may not save life because we cannot destroy it." But an increasing number of thinkers — those she was counting on to mold public opinion in the end — were coming to agree with Henry White of Kansas, who declared that it was not to raise the moral tone, or to purify politics, or to improve municipal conditions, or to raise wages, that woman suffrage was demanded. All these would probably follow. But the question was one of *rights*.

It was about this time that Edward Everett Hale said there were two messages he never failed to read: the President's message to Congress and Miss Willard's to her constituency.

That fall the W.C.T.U. held its convention in the Metropolitan Opera House, New York, " one of the five largest halls in the world." The deliberations of its four hundred and ten delegates lasted five days. Its program covered fourteen printed pages; forty departments reported progress; fifty officers were elected. For an audience " five thousand strong " there was a program of one hundred and eighty-two items, including lectures on dress reform and cooking; there were flag presentations, introduction of notable visitors, and music by the White-Ribbon Quartette. Someone called the convention a " moral jumbo."

Mrs. Mary T. Burt had had the temerity to rent so costly an auditorium, and the business head to serve free lunches daily to the delegates, paying for them and the Opera House by the sale of seats and boxes to the general public. Madame Demorest, who had made a fortune as America's foremost fashion designer, paid for the decoration of the house. Moreover, she gave a reception to delegates, at which were present Clara Barton of the Red Cross, Jennie June, widely read columnist, Anna Howard Shaw, preacher and suffragist, and several prominent Prohibitionists.

On this stage only a few months before had sat magisterially the Methodists who declined to admit Frances Willard and three other women delegates to the General Conference. But remembrance of that incident caused Miss Willard only a momentary qualm in the presence of these women who were eager to hasten the coming of the " Republic of God," in which " no mere accident of color, race, sex or nationality " was a bar to perfect equality.

With Mrs. Thompson of Hillsboro, a crusader now very frail, the women read responsively the Crusade psalm from the Hillsboro Bible, and sang the Crusade hymn, " Give to the Winds Thy Fears." And Frances Willard, looking back fifteen years to the days of the Crusade, thought, " What hath God wrought! "

As usual, a woman preached the annual sermon. This year

it was Grace Greenwood of Brooklyn. She was followed by Bishop Fallows, Reformed Episcopal church leader of Chicago, who contended for the "Ecclesiastical Emancipation of Women" (let the conservative Methodist bishops read and consider).

The president proposed the installation of white-ribbon deaconesses, trained for evangelistic work by Bible scholars of repute, and for nursing by the Union's National Temperance Hospital. Thus they would be fitted to preach, teach, and act as visiting nurses — a work sadly needed. She felt there were thousands of women, young and old, who would gladly dedicate themselves to such service. And, recurring to a favorite theme of hers, she added, "What the world needs is mothering, most of all in the church."

But not all was harmony. There was a discordant note of which the papers made much. Mrs. J. Ellen Foster of Iowa was protesting vigorously, even acrimoniously, against alignment with the Prohibition party. She was alarmed by the defections from the ranks of Republican sympathizers.

To Frances Willard it had not mattered that for years her Union had hesitated to follow her into politics. She could wait. What did matter was that her old and tried friend Ellen Foster led the opposition — Ellen Foster, by whose side she had fought in so many battles. Now they were in opposite camps, and neither could hope that the other would yield. The split was permanent. Once during the controversy Miss Willard was moved to bitter tears, the first she had shed since she left Northwestern.

In 1880, when Miss Willard had urged a strong prohibition policy (though not as yet allied with the Prohibition party), Mrs. Foster had voiced no objection. Four years later, however, when Miss Willard (then a Prohibitionist) had asked her "sisters " to follow, Mrs. Foster had braced herself for a fight to the finish for the Republican party, which had given Iowa a prohibition constitutional amendment. Year after year for four years, she had presented a resolution favoring nonpartisanship. Each year Prohibitionists had multiplied, while her own following had decreased, till in 1888 it was negligible. In appreciation of her loyalty the Republicans had made her chairman of their Woman's National Committee.

Some urged that she be dropped as vice-president of the W.C.T.U. But Miss Willard, natural peacemaker, pleaded against pettiness and for their bond of sisterhood. " Envy and jealousy," she warned, " light the intensest fires that ever burn in human hearts." So Mrs. Foster remained in office. But her power in the National Union was at an end, while Frances Willard, general, politician, peacemaker, sat more secure than ever.

In the spring of 1888, President and Mrs. Cleveland entertained a new organization — the Woman's International Council, with Susan B. Anthony as president and Frances Willard as one of the founders. A National Council was created for America. On Miss Anthony's insistence, Miss Willard was elected president, an honor she attributed to her friend's " generous partiality."

But, after death had parted them, that friend could not find praise strong enough for Miss Willard: " She was a most remarkable, a most extraordinary woman in every respect . . . masterly . . . a great general . . . superintended every branch of her work. She was a bunch of magnetism, possessing that occult force which all leaders must have. . . . She had a great depth of understanding." Elizabeth Stuart Phelps (Ward), friend of them both, thought Miss Willard had not been sufficiently appreciated "as an intellect." "Spirituality without intellectuality," she said, "could not have moved the forces that obeyed the motions of her beautiful hand. . . . She will long illustrate the value of educated consecration." So it would seem Miss Anthony's "partiality" had a very sound basis.

The Council seems to have been only another expression of the "do-everything" policy of the W.C.T.U., another means of securing solidarity among women of every race and type. Its aim was to win by numbers the passage of laws for the betterment of women and children. Three new goals were the placement of women on school and library boards and boards charged with the care of defectives. "Mothering" was Miss Willard's name for woman's part in government. Years later, Mary McDowell, seeking civic reforms, called it "good housekeeping in government."

"God made woman with all her faculties and her way of looking at things," said the National Council's president, "to be a helpmate to man. I like to see how grandly men are meeting the uprising of womanhood. It is not to keep us down that men do not let us enter politics. They are waiting for us to be a little more anxious. They are waiting themselves to get wonted to the notion." And to the men she said, "I do not forget that, *if* we come, *you and you only* must open the door."

How confident she was that she would see the hinges turn and roll wide the door of the twentieth century to let the women in! She should have lived till then; she would have been only seventy-one. But she burned her candle at both ends. It was consumed before the twentieth century was ushered in.

In the early eighties, the W.C.T.U. had given its hard-working president a cottage in the Catskills, where she could be refreshed by the beauty she loved. Friends furnished it. She

Oliver Willard

and

Mary B. Willard

Madam Willard

Anna Gordon

Lady Henry Somerset

named it the "Eagle's Nest." But so long as Madam Willard lived, she spent the short three-weeks' vacation in Evanston. One summer after her mother's death, she and Lady Henry took a brief outing at Eagle's Nest. But even then she could not escape work. All day she sat bent over her desk, with her back to the window, lest the witchery of the mountains distract her from business. Sometimes she burned her candle at both ends, and tapped the middle for a third wick to burn.

(XIII)

After Fifty Years

"WRITE THE STORY OF YOUR LIFE," BEGGED HER FRIENDS, "TO celebrate your fiftieth birthday." Often before they had asked for an autobiography, but Miss Willard was "averse" to the idea. Here however was a special occasion, a fixed date, for the book. "But we want a true story," they said, "not one that tells only half the truth through fear of seeming egotistical."

For years these friends had followed her lead, done her bidding. How could she longer refuse this one request? Reluctantly she consented. But how to find the time was the question. If Satan ever found mischief for her to do, it was not because of idle hands. Her correspondence of thousands of letters a year was only a pastime; trains were her home, lecture halls and committee rooms her goals.

Time passed, and she had made little progress. The deadline was near, beyond which she might not delay. She looked about for a retreat from her madding world. What, after all, she reflected, is more isolated than a hotel room in the heart of a great city? So to Chicago she went.

Nothing better demonstrates the high tension at which she worked than the bulk of the manuscript with which she emerged at the end of three months — some six hundred thousand words, twelve hundred printed quarto pages! Handing it to the publishers (the Woman's Temperance Publication Association), she said in effect, "Here it is, written not as I would but as I could. It may do good [the decisive argument]. At all events, you asked for it."

Six hundred thousand words; twelve hundred pages! Childhood, girlhood, college, teaching, travel — the story rippled from the tip of her pen. Not till she reached "reformer" and "politician" did the speed slacken, as befitted a serious subject. Then a short sketch of the W.C.T.U.'s aims and evolution. That done, she was free to slip again into chatty pages, delightful in their glimpses of people, most delightful in glimpses of herself. "No one ever so completely turned himself inside out for the benefit of his readers," says Bradford with amusement. But Mrs. Hannah Whitall Smith, who wrote the preface, reminds us that it was written "*by request of* and *for* the women of whom Miss Willard is the beloved leader; if others see it, that is their own good fortune." "Written for the great family circle," it is to be read by those who love the writer.

The writer knew — none better — that the book was loosely strung together. How could it have been otherwise? Six hundred thousand words, ten times the number in most books, always written in haste, between jumps! For that reason she gave it the title *Glimpses of Fifty Years*. The publishers cut the twelve hundred pages to seven hundred (with keen regret), but absolved Miss Willard of all responsibility for the material discarded.

"Silhouettes," she calls the delightful compôte with which she ends the book — two hundred pages of anecdotes, sketches of interesting people, her views on many subjects, a self-analysis which, rightly understood, is so helpful to an understanding of her career. Like all her writings, it suffers from haste. She whose ambition it had been to write never had time to revise anything she had written. But her joy in adventuring with life gives the autobiography a savor revision might have spoiled.

Perhaps a precious memory has been overlooked. She tucks it in here. Such is the picture of carrying on the Fourth the first American flag she had ever seen, made from an old pillow-case, strips of turkey-red and tinsel stars. Another is of three children perched precariously on the roof of the barn to watch rockets shoot skyward from Janesville, six miles away. Somewhere she pays tribute to her dog "Prohibition" ("Hibbie" for short; "Hib" for shorter).

There is the anecdote of going to Amesbury to urge the school ballot for women, only to be told by a group of women, "Oh, yes, we women vote in Amesbury. Mr. Whittier wishes it." Or again, of being sidetracked for twelve hours on her return from speaking in New Orleans. The only woman in the Pullman, she sat absorbed in writing. Suddenly came the realization of how hungry those men must be. Her hostess had furnished her a sumptuous lunch. Setting it forth temptingly, she invited the men to share it. Quickly they gathered round her. One fetched boiling water from the engineer's cab; another made the coffee; she furnished sugar and cream. The way was open now for conversation. The wife of one was in the W.C.T.U.; another had heard Miss Willard speak once; a third had just heard her twice in New Orleans. Altogether, it was a happy occasion.

Here emerges her threefold creed — social, industrial, and religious — the structure of belief that had grown through the years. The center of society is the home, with father, mother, and children; not to be confused with an upholstered model, but "a place conscious of benignity." The wife will have proved before marriage her ability to earn a living. She will have married for love, not for bread and butter. Home duties will be so equalized as to create more tenderness in the husband, more poise and equanimity in the wife. "An undivided half apiece for wife and husband; coeducation to mate them on the plane of mind; equal property rights to make her God's own free woman, not coerced into marriage for the sake of a support, nor a bond-slave who asks her master for the price of a paper of pins and gives him back the change." Some day "the wife shall surrender at marriage no right not equally surrendered by the husband — not even her own name!" Elsewhere she speaks of George Eliot as the first woman to attain the post mortem honor of having her husband publicly called her "widower."

For the children, the public schools shall be the training ground, to teach them, first and foremost, the laws of their being — diet, dress, exercise, sleep — and good manners. Why not? Why music and art, lists of prepositions, the rivers of Tibet, and not the laws of their being? Why not ethics, the basis of all culture? But the bedrock of all their learning must be natural law, with free discussion and experiment. They must be taught the effects of alcohol, but always from a scientific standpoint. Patriotism must be ingrained. Intelligent citizenship must be the goal. As part of public education should come the teaching of vocations. In *How to Win* she urges girls to be good for something, to use their talents for the common welfare, to be specialists. There is not a thing men can do that women should not be urged to try.

Her religion was simple Christianity. "Our bodies are just as sacred as our spirits." Knowing God would solve the temperance, the labor, and the woman questions, and Christ's philosophy would become the center of education. She called faith "God's dynamite," and joy "the outcome of balanced faculties." She believed that, if faith and prayer were reduced to scientific terms, thousands whom the church does not now reach would lay hold on them. "We have consecrated our knees to Him," she writes, "when it was our hands He wanted. . . . God is ACTION. Let us be like God."

Her economic creed naturally fitted into the religious: "I

believe in the reign of the common people; that the earth is theirs and everything in it; that the kingdom of heaven is going to be here; that through the gospel there is to be a warmer glow of love. . . . I believe that there will be no private property, no private opportunities of education and culture, but that each human being will desire to have every other human being enjoy to the utmost comfort, development and cultivation."

She uses the two hands to illustrate the two forces of capital and labor: the left less skilled, served often by its fellow, and decked with rings; the right, forceful and ingenious, busy, unadorned. Only by their acting together can a full day's toil be accomplished. Acting together, they bring social solidarity; opposed, they but mar and destroy the social fabric. "And the left hand of capital," she warns, "will first give way under the pitiless blows of labor's strong right hand." Radical, even dangerous, doctrines these in her day.

In her acquaintance she numbered many well known writers: Whittier, Whitman, Harris, Lanier, Haynes, Harriet Beecher Stowe, two women owners and editors of outstanding New Orleans papers — Mrs. Herrick of the *Picayune* and Mrs. Field of the *Times-Democrat*. Writers always had a peculiar attraction for her. Oliver's years as owner and editor of a daily and her own short experience as his successor had instilled an admiration for newspaper men; she was convinced that the journalistic temperament was about the finest in the world.

Until the bitter controversy over woman suffrage and the Prohibition party, she had been generally accorded generous consideration by the press. She attributed the changed attitude of the papers partly to the editorial love of dramatizing. At all events, she now saw a dreadful pen-and-ink dragon in the chair of the once genial editor.

Of course, she had done plenty of writing herself — paragraphs, articles, books. That was, in a sense, her business. Always they were written in haste, by snatches. Once after her return from abroad, *Harper's* had taken an article, the *Century* a letter. The height of her ambition had been to make the *Atlantic*. She knew now that she never would. That she had made many " lesser lights " did not console her. A friend had said once of her work, " How much better, if she could take more time! " She knew the truth of this — that only the " unhasting " pen can create that which shall not die.

In the section " People I have Met " she gives delightful reminiscences of Henry Ward Beecher who was a hero of Madam Willard's and author of the *Letters to Young Men*, which she had given her son as a safeguard when he left home for college. In 1880, Beecher became a convert to the ballot for woman, and introduced Miss Willard to a Brooklyn audience. When she had finished her lecture he remounted the rostrum, shook her hand heartily, and faced the audience with, " And yet *she can't vote!* "

Among remarkable women she lists Elizabeth Rodgers, Master Workman of District No. 24, Chicago, whom she took the time to look up and interview. The first Chicago woman to join the Knights of Labor, Mrs. Rodgers, encouraged by her husband, had risen to the head of a union of three hundred men. Fortnightly, this comely woman of forty, mother of ten children and her own housekeeper, presided at the meetings, careful never to let the men catch her making a mistake in her duties. She had no time to prepare a speech, but she was a naturally ready speaker, mentally alert, with a concise and pointed style. Recalling the interview, Miss Willard again pays tribute to the Knights, whose local assembly in every town drew young men away from the saloon, while the debates made them more intelligent citizens. Through ostracizing saloonkeepers and investors in the liquor business, labor was doing more for temperance, said she, than the propagandists of her own Union.

Not the least interesting of the " Silhouettes " is the account of her education in public speaking through hearing and apprais-ing other women speakers. First, there was the Abolitionist of the forties, who defied the traditions of her sex and chose a theme that might well have incited to mob violence. Next was the Spiritualist in Milwaukee, whom Frank went to hear in spite of Aunt Sarah's protests. The woman looked queer and pitiful, suspended somehow between floor and ceiling. But one of her sentences remained in Frank's memory for life: " I love to think about a central peace subsisting at the heart of endless agitation." In time Frank was to attain that peace.

The third speaker was Anna Dickinson, eloquent suffragist, whom she first heard speak during the war in Crosby Opera House, Chicago's pride. The city's most distinguished citizens sat on the platform. Again Frank forgot everything that was said; but the radiant personality, the dark curls, the eyes that " mirrored immortality," the vibrant voice, stirred her deeply. She and Miss Dickinson became fast friends, though Miss Dick-inson declined to join the Temperance Union.

It was after Miss Willard's return from abroad that she made her own first public appearance. A gray-haired man who had heard her in missionary meetings and thought she had " the art of putting things " asked her to talk in fashionable Centenary Methodist Church, Chicago, of which he was a trustee. Bol-stered by his confidence and his official position, she spoke " be-fore the elite of the city." So hearty was the applause that she felt she had found her field. Four years later she entered on her career as a platform speaker. Yet she never ceased to have a sense of immense responsibility for making worth while the time an audience gave her.

Last in her autobiography comes that self-revelation her friends had hoped might help others. She admits she is ambitious: "I always wanted to react upon the world to my utmost ounce of power." Yet she could say truthfully that she had never sought power; "advancement" had always come to her unasked. "What mind I have is intuitional," she continues; "such facilities as I have are always on hand. What I do must be done quickly." She had no strong antipathies. But "not to be jealous of others who come at rattling pace along the track, speeding onward neck and neck, or distancing one's self altogether, is a difficult grace. I do not profess to have attained it."

And what of reformers? When a reformer stands alone, she has found, he is a "fanatic"; when there are several with him, they are "enthusiasts"; when everybody is with him, he is a "hero." But the real heroes are the workers of the rank and file. "Theirs the small round of duties, the weary toil, the valor without renown." And in one of her frequent bursts of gratitude to her followers, she witnesses to "the unselfish devotion that glories to see its leader's name writ large, and upbears him in faithful arms when he is wounded."

But oh, the loneliness of leadership! That "infinite remoteness from every being save God! . . . The leader is first to draw the enemy's fire. He is held responsible for the failures of his following, for their mutinies and marplots. Their random blows strike him ofttimes rather than the enemy. It may be said of him (on the human plane), 'He saved others; himself he cannot save.'" The mountaintop was, indeed, a lonely place, but peace dwelt there. On the plain below, her mother's prophecy was fulfilled — "It will be yours to wrestle, not to reign."

It did not lessen her loneliness that Mary B. and her daughters, Katharine and Mamie, now lived abroad, or that Oliver's sons were fast disintegrating. Their disintegration was only an added spur to her to save others.

A well known critic has said that every man's personality should be thought of as a house of many rooms, some of which are lighted for all to see, while others are retreats where the soul can brood, and dream, and grow. Obliging as Frances Willard was in opening an unusual number of rooms to the public, one cannot doubt there were some she kept safeguarded — sacred forever.

"A bright day in a bright life," read the headline of the Evanston *Press* announcing the celebration of Miss Willard's fiftieth birthday, September 28, 1889. Evanston's testimonial was to be a surprise to her famous daughter. Hence the *Press* did not announce it till the morning of the twenty-eighth, and care was taken that Rest Cottage did not get its copy. But the mistress of the cottage had plenty of reminders that this was her birthday. They began with Hannah's poking her head in at the door, to wish her many happy returns. Letters and telegrams poured in, gifts piled up, old neighbors called. The Band of Hope marched to her door, and carried her off to enjoy their Harvest Home. At noon twelve ladies toasted her and her mother, and "our absent men friends, who make our lives so happy."

In the evening, they wheedled her to the Methodist church on some pretext, and got her on the platform. Not till she faced a thousand friends old and new and their applause did she realize that this was her home-town's tribute to her. The president of the village presided. President Cummings of Northwestern recalled her influence for good as dean of women. The W.C.T.U. and the Woman's Council had sent speakers. Ministers and leading citizens joined in praise of her. There were choruses by the Loyal Legion, and solos by girls she had known from babyhood. Messages were read from John Greenleaf Whittier, Susan B. Anthony, Lyman Abbott, former President Hayes, and others, followed by resolutions and good wishes.

Now it was time for her to say something. She spoke with her usual simplicity and play of humor, said the *Press,* yet with deep feeling, and with that " subtle magnetism " that was hers. This was the most wonderful day in all her tolerably lengthy existence, she said — like a fairy tale — and she liked fairy tales. She had been too much a recluse among them. She was going to reform. She had resolved that henceforth she would keep open house one afternoon a week whenever she was in Evanston. Would they not drop in? She would feel " a little sorrowful " if they didn't. As proof of her sincerity, there survives a calling card with " Saturday " in the lower left-hand corner. She did not remind them that as president of the National and the World's W.C.T.U. and of the National Woman's Council, as head of the White Cross, national Prohibition committeeman, and writer of thousands of letters a year, she had little time left for chatting with her neighbors, however dear. She thanked them for this proof of their love, and pledged hers in return.

Why on such a joyous occasion should she have ended impulsively with the prayer " Lead, Kindly Light "? It was as if she glimpsed a shadow around the corner, a shadow that would cloud all the days to come. Instantly, however, she was again radiant, assuring them all that Evanston's testimonial had meant more to her than she could express in her most fervent thanks. The W.C.T.U. would fête her as a matter of course. But the loyalty of Evanston, the " dearest place on earth," she had sometimes doubted. Now that it had shown its affection and appreciation, she was supremely happy. It was the perfect end of a perfect day. And the day had been none the less perfect because on the committee of arrangements had been " her " Mary Jones, widow of Professor, the founder and president of her alma mater. For Mrs. Jones and her daughter she had cleared the " Annex " in which Mary B. and her children had lived for seven years after Oliver's death. The merry countenance of Mary Jones was a constant reminder of college days, when life had begun to take on a meaning and a plan.

Five years later, after the death of her own mother, she was to write Mrs. Jones' daughter Lydia:

" My dear Lillie Jones:

Coming home last night I learned that my dear teacher of other and friend of all the years since I was eighteen has suddenly left you, her only daughter, for the better world. Since then I have dwelt mostly in the memory of the happy days given to me and many another by those brave, true spirits, William and Mary, who were king and queen of our young hearts when life was in its joyous morning. I have seen the dear old college, the shady grounds, the smiling faces at the windows, the fragrant Commencement days in the old church, you and Willie as little children playing about — a fair, bright picture without a shade to mar its charm. . . . And I who know now what it is to lose a mother tender and true, reach out my hand to you in loving loyalty to *them* and to *you,* and pray that God's comfort may rest upon your heart as it has come to rest on mine. . . ."

The family at Rest Cottage had hardly had time to recover from the celebration before the W.C.T.U. convention met in Chicago, when women from all over the United States joined in doing honor to their chief. Madam Willard was there, and later received eight hundred guests at her home.

They held jubilation over Miss Willard's autobiography, whose title page bore the legend, " Written by order of the

Woman's Christian Temperance Union." Despite protests, the author formally made over to the Union all royalties after the illustrations were paid for. Thus the book entered upon its long and steady sale.

While adulation was being poured upon its president, the Union was being played up by the press in spectacular fashion. A story that easily lent itself to dramatization was the renewal of Mrs. Foster's fight for nonpartisanship. The Union also came in for badgering because of its support of woman suffrage, "repulsive to all sensible men and a stone around the neck of the Prohibition party."

The Chicago *Daily News,* as usual, came to Miss Willard's defense. If, said the editor, she was indeed as impractical as her opponents claimed, the hundreds of clever women she led would surely have found it out long since. The world had need of more women as impractical as she, for every saloonkeeper knew the power of her Union.

For days the "Foster-Willard Fight" was front-page news. When at last Mrs. Foster and her followers made a dramatic exit from the hall, Miss Willard immediately called other Iowa women to fill the seats vacated, and introduced Mrs. Carhart as chairman of the new delegation. So ended the long struggle between the onetime "wheel-horses" of the National Union.

Commenting on Mrs. Foster's action, the *News* said, "The little girl took her playthings and went home because she couldn't be the 'mother.'"

But the storm of applause that greeted Miss Willard as she rose to make her annual address was heartening. What with the weakening of prohibition states, she had been as near discouragement as she ever got. The cloud passed. During the declamation contest of young women for the Demorest diamond medal, no one was more radiant than the president.

The prospect — once the Foster-Willard strife was forgotten — had never been brighter for harmony and unimpeded progress. A department of peace and international arbitration was created, and another to push physical education. The latter worked in well with scientific temperance education, which, under Mrs. Hunt, was meeting with success among adults as well as in the schools.

Strong allies in temperance education were insurance statistics, which showed the longevity of the total abstainer to be from thirty to forty per cent greater than that of the moderate drinker. Nor could one ignore the testimony — and physicians were not ignoring it — of so eminent a medical man as Dr. N. S. Davis of Evanston and Chicago, who after long experiment had discontinued the use of alcoholic stimulants, convinced that his patients made a better recovery without them. In England, Sir Thomas Barlow, physician to the future King Edward VII, urged total abstinence, not as fanaticism or asceticism, but as "rational self-control in respect to something fraught with untold risks." Coaches in athletics had no use for "whisky nerves" or "beer-weakened muscles."

Henry Justin Smith dubs Miss Willard "a nation-wide proselyter." Her portrait hung in thousands of homes — "portrait of a lady with severe eyeglasses but gentle expression, . . . the greatest celebrity among Chicago women of the nineties," when the saloon had become "a burning question."

In a drink-cursed world, this "proselyter" was trying to create what psychologists today call a new behavior pattern.

(XIV)

The Great Divide

THE YEAR 1891 MARKED THE END OF AN EPOCH. FRANCES WILLARD ceased to belong to America alone and became an international figure. The change was marked by the first biennial convention of the World's W.C.T.U., its first really world-wide gathering of women of many nationalities, colors, creeds. They met in historic Faneuil Hall, Boston, which had been decorated in dramatic fashion. The walls and the platform were hung with hundreds of yards of white muslin, its edges bound in red and blue, the favorite colors in the flags of the world. On the muslin were pasted a million and a half signatures to Miss Willard's Polyglot Petition, in every type of chirography, from Chinese ideographs and flowing Sanskrit to the cross and the fingerprint. Against this background floated flags of all nations. On platform and tables were plants of every clime.

If there had been any fear lest this first international meeting lack the dignity of numbers, that fear turned to delight as crowds choked the aisles and overflowed into the street. The crowd had come to hear Frances Willard — so said the papers — and would not be denied. On the platform with Miss Willard sat Lady Henry Somerset, president of the British Women's Temperance Association, and other leaders from Great Britain, Australia, Newfoundland, from Italy and South America, from Japan, China and Hawaii. At the first convention, in 1874, but seventeen states had been represented. Now there were delegates from fifty-one American states and territories, as well as from other countries. The Union had organized fifty nations, "Christian and pagan."

Since Lady Henry Somerset was in America for the first time, few knew of her work for better housing among the tenants of her great estate or of her philanthropies in London. But after Miss Willard had praised her level head, her warm heart and her helpful hand, the audience stood, gave the Chautauqua salute of fluttering handkerchiefs, and sang "God Save the Queen." Then Miss Willard turned over the meeting to Lady Henry. A simple courtesy, yet it opened the door to the most significant period in their two lives. No one — they least of all — guessed the significance of their mutual attraction at first sight — that in it had germinated what was to become a famous international friendship almost romantic in its intensity. "Chivalric," one has called it, "symbol of a new form of friendship beginning to bind good women together the world over." Through it, "the lonely worker loses the sense of isolation," takes heart, becomes more understanding. Herein, said the press, lay Miss Willard's greatest power — "in her peculiar genius for friendship among all sorts and conditions of life." And one "sort" was Chicago reporters. From now on, whether they liked her doctrines or not, they liked her, and gave friendly reports of her conventions.

One of the chief acts of that convention was to vote to send the Polyglot Petition to the rulers of the fifty nations represented by its signers. Translated into dozens of languages, with the signatures photographed, it was now ready to be sent to the potentates. It asked for better homes and happier through the abolition of liquor and narcotics. Though the rulers might ignore it, it would rally the women of the world around a common standard, and it voiced their protest against social evils.

When Miss Willard had been elected president the World's

W.C.T.U. adjourned to join the W.C.T.U. of America for a week of earnest work. But not till it had accepted Mrs. Potter Palmer's invitation to hold its next convention in Chicago, in connection with the World's Columbian Exposition.

In the summer of 1892, the W.C.T.U. celebrated Anna Gordon's birthday on the lawn of Rest Cottage. Madam Willard looked down from the second floor balcony, and once rose feebly to acknowledge greetings to herself. Life for her was almost done. Two weeks later, on August 6, her body was laid beside her husband's at Rosehill. Her granddaughter Katharine pictures those last days very graphically:

"That summer, for the first time in sixty years of housekeeping, my grandmother gave up the place at the head of the table, and transferred the duties of that position in her gracious way to me. . . . In July she stopped coming down, and the whole life of the house suddenly centered in the one room upstairs where she was. She said that she was 'worn out' with the heat and her eighty-eight years, and that there was 'no sense' in trying to eat what she did not need." Then, gradually, it "got to be the natural thing that she should not rise in the morning, and finally . . . that grandma would not get up at all . . . there was 'no sense' in wasting her strength on such hot days." She had always hoped her passing "might make death a less terrible thing to those who should be with her. And here am I to testify that, for the first time in my life, death cast no shadow over me; I could realize nothing but the beautiful significance of that passing from death unto life."

Miss Willard had had one of the new phonographs installed in her mother's room — the "Chamber of Peace," they named it — to record the sayings witty and wise, the last precious words, of "Saint Courageous." To Frank Madam Willard confided that the coming of Lady Henry Somerset had "lighted the whole world" for her. "God sent her as much on my account as for your sake," she said, "and the sake of the cause . . . that I might leave the world in peace." She had dreaded the thought of living to be ninety, yet for Frank's sake she must stay. But now, she continued, Lady Henry "will not only give you the strength that I could not at my age, but she will give you the love and sympathy without which you could not live. . . . I never think of you and Anna as separate; I expect you always to go on together. But to breast the waves of this great reform, who can so well keep step with you as Lady Henry, for you are in perfect harmony." Then, in that whimsical fashion of hers, she added, "You could not have planned for this to be so, if you had tried a thousand years. God had to do it, and he did it."

There was a word too for Kate Jackson: "God sent you when we needed you most." To Dr. Bragdon — whose father had been Evanston's first minister and the Willards' next-door neighbor for over thirty years — she said, "You have done all you could. If you can get a balloon and start it for heaven, I will step on board with alacrity. Give my love to your mother." And when he protested they wouldn't let her go yet, she answered, "But the Lord is going to get ahead of you, Met." So she joked to the last.

The phonograph recorded her last prayer: "We walk out into the mystery fearless, because we trust in Thee. We face the great emergency with our hearts full of vital questions that cannot here be answered. We leave them all with Thee. . . . We would know many things that Thou hast not revealed, but we can only love — and trust — and wait."

The Methodist church was filled with friends come to pay their last tribute. On the casket lay three palm leaves tied with white ribbon inscribed " From Frank," and a heart of roses and ferns which Lady Henry had sent to the " Saint Courageous." The active pallbearers were men of prominence in Evanston and the university. Of the honorary women pallbearers, two represented the W.C.T.U.; the other four had been Madam Willard's neighbors for thirty years and more. At Rosehill, the casket was lowered into a grave lined with evergreen from Forest Home.

Among her mother's papers, the daughter found a clipping with a poem entitled " Alone in the House," long treasured by one who had never made complaint because she was so much alone. Now in her own bitter loneliness that daughter faced again the question, " Does death end all? " Then came to her the thought: " Suppose a man should build a ship and freight it with the rarest works of art, and in the very building should plan to convey the ship out into mid-ocean and there scuttle it with all its contents! And here is the human body, in itself an admirable piece of mechanism, the most delicate and wonderful of which we know. It is like a splendid ship, but its cargo incomparably outruns the value of itself, for it is made up of love, hope, veneration, imagination, and all the largess of man's unconquerable mind. Why should its Maker scuttle such a ship with such a freightage? "

Two years later appeared *A Great Mother,* by Frances Willard and her kinswoman Minerva Brace Norton. Its many sketches by friends make a composite which the *Advance* called " the record of a rare, sweet soul."

Three weeks after Madam Willard's death, Miss Willard — a mere shadow of herself, worn by long watches — sailed with Miss Gordon for England, to be the guest of Lady Henry Somerset, whom the devoted mother had recognized as her own inevitable successor. The years that followed were to put to the test the unselfishness of Miss Gordon's adoration — for such it was — for the woman to whom she had dedicated her life. Generously she stepped aside to let this new, invigorating friendship rekindle their leader's torch. To Lady Henry's "sustaining love and care" she credits the prolonging of Miss Willard's life.

To a friend, Miss Willard wrote from England: "We are keeping very quiet here, seeing no one, receiving shoals of letters from all parts of the Kingdom as well as from 'home, sweet home.' For myself, I am not very vigorous, but am grinding away at my annual address, though with but little enthusiasm, since mother is not here."

For the first time in her life she knew luxury and ease. She had earned them. There had been long years of the most rigid economy, years of uninterrupted activity. Miss Stewart, an American caller, pictures the two friends reclining in great armchairs before the fire, sipping their after-dinner coffee. Miss Willard was her natural self, though richly dressed in a pale blue gown, its Elizabethan ruff forming a frame for her "classic" head with its wavy gold-brown hair. Pale satin with creamy lace set off Lady Henry's dark beauty. "The warmth and cordiality of their greeting, the delight of their conversation, the richness and glow of their surroundings, made an ineffaceable impression."

In the fall, Lady Henry returned with her friend to America for the National W.C.T.U. convention at Denver. Then together they journeyed back to England.

For England's welcome to Frances Willard that winter of 1892, Lady Henry chose Exeter Hall. Five thousand gathered in the historic building; for those not fortunate enough to get in, the program was repeated in another hall. On the platform sat philanthropists, members of Parliament, London county councilors, church dignitaries, temperance and labor leaders. Protestant, Catholic and Jew united to do her honor. Masonic lodges, guilds and unions sent greeting.

On her entrance the audience rose, waved handerchiefs à la Chautauqua and gave three lusty British cheers beyond anything the visitor had ever heard in volume. Lady Henry introduced her; Canon Wilberforce of Westminster gave the first of a score of welcomes. The guest rose to reply.

Never before, said she, had she been more pleased to be able to trace her "undiluted ancestry" back nine generations to an honest yeoman of Kent. The English, who had seemed to her heretofore too reticent, now as an audience seemed to "bloom like a garden bed." She spoke on the modern temperance movement, and explained her Union's "do-everything" policy as threefold: "The liquor traffic is entrenched in the customs of society — go after it with the pledge of total abstinence for the sake of others. The liquor traffic is protected by people's ignorance — go after it in the schools. The liquor traffic is safeguarded by law — go after it in the legislature." And she added, "There are two serpents, intemperance and impurity. . . . The two must rise or fall together."

One paper reporting the meeting said no one had evoked a more universal interest or received a greater ovation. The *Review of Reviews* headed its sketch of her, "The Uncrowned Queen of American Democracy." The London *Daily News,* organ of the liberal party, spoke of her eloquence unadorned, her quaint Americanisms, her quiet earnestness, her dry humor, and her common sense, as having a wonderful effect upon the audience. Even the *Spectator,* while lamenting the "fanaticism" of temperance women in general, acknowledged Miss Willard had done much good in her own country.

When frazzled nerves had been sufficiently repaired and poise restored, Lady Henry took her guest on what proved to be a triumphal tour, including every important city of Great Britain and Ireland. All vied in the heartiness of their welcome. " Josiah Flynt " says that after the meeting at Edinburgh enthusiastic students unhitched the horses and pulled his aunt's carriage to her hotel.

All this adulation was thrilling, but the " distinguished guest " paid a high price for her " dance." When the time arrived for the second biennial convention of the World's W.C.T.U., at Chicago's Columbian Exposition, the world president was too ill to attend. Physicians ordered rest, absolute rest. Rest for Frances Willard! So while Lady Henry, accompanied by Anna Gordon, did duty for her in Chicago, the invalid rested at Haslemere, England, the country home of Hannah Whitall Smith.

In Chicago's Art Institute, linked with the Columbian Exposition, gathered women from many lands for the convention of the World's W.C.T.U. A reporter inclined to be cynical eyed the audience critically, then decided that here was " emphatically a gathering of earnest, thoughtful women " he had better treat seriously. He waited. The clapping of gloved hands made him sit up and take notice. Down the aisle swept " a woman of gracious appearance " gowned in black lace, a purple-lined mantle across her shoulders. Lady Henry Somerset, he heard them say — the vice-president-at-large who was to preside. She took her seat under a globe representing the earth and encircled with white ribbons. Below that hung the Union's motto, " For God and Home and Every Land." On desks and platform were bowls of roses red and white.

In a popular mid-Victorian story, the little drudge sighs, " So many good times in the world and I ain't in 'em!" This was one of the best of times, and Frances Willard wasn't in it! In fourteen years as national president she had missed but one day. But, rest or no rest, she *had* written her annual address, which Lady Henry would read.

First, however, there were many official welcomes from the Exposition: from President Bonney, heading the numerous congresses, many of whose foreign delegates would address the Temperance Union; from Mrs. Potter Palmer, president of the Board of Lady Managers, and Mrs. Charles Henrotin, her chief of staff; from Archbishop Ireland representing the Catholic Church; from Susan B. Anthony representing the suffragists. Said Archbishop Ireland: "Among the many congresses which during the last four or five months have assembled in this place, yours is one of the most important. . . . So long as intemperance prevails, *battles of reform in every direction will necessarily be fruitless,* for intemperance destroys reason and loosens the barriers which God has constructed to resist vice and sin."

Miss Willard's address called attention to what the Exposition meant to womankind. Never before had such provision been made for them: they were directors; they were on committees of award; great women were honored equally with great men, the Woman's Congress was attracting hundreds there.

Mrs. Hunt, of the Union's education department, reported that the forty-fourth state had adopted a law requiring education in temperance in the public schools. For years she had employed trained workers in her laboratories and enlisted specialists to write textbooks. By 1901 the forty-eighth state would wheel into line. During the year the Union had lost two of its oldest and most valued workers: Mary Allen West, long editor of the *Union Signal,* and Jennie Cassidy, who for twenty of her thirty bedridden years had directed the Flower Mission.

The most surprising event connected with the convention was the Chicago *Tribune's* three columns of advance information, reviewing the history of the W.C.T.U. and citing statistics for the United States. These showed a hundred sixty thousand members in the parent society, two hundred thousand in the Loyal Legion of young people, and twenty thousand in the "Y's." The locals numbered ten thousand.

The convention was most successful, though Miss Willard was missed. All sang her praises. Lady Henry spoke of her triumphal tour through Great Britain and Ireland, of her work in helping to reorganize the British Women's Temperance Association along American lines. The white-ribboners at home began to realize that Frances Willard was no longer exclusively theirs, that she now belonged to the world. Recognition of that fact must explain much of what was to follow.

American white-ribboners of the nineties knew little of the Englishwoman whose friendship Miss Willard characterized as the most beautiful that had ever blessed her life. Had they known her better, they would not have harbored that feeling of jealousy because their president was so happy outside her native land.

When Lady Henry had married Lord Henry Somerset, heir to the dukedom of Beaufort, in 1872, she was already noted for her charm and was a belle among belles. After two happy years a son was born. Then came revelations that she as wife and mother could not ignore, and that his parents felt to be disgraceful. She did not believe in divorce; she must ask for a legal separation. But to secure it she must openly prefer charges against her husband, a proceeding held to be so indelicate in a lady that instantly the doors of her social world closed against her. It was the only world she knew, and she loved it. Its glitter, its self-indulgence, its pageantry appealed to her inherited tastes. Quietly she retired with her four-year-old boy to Reigate Priory on her father's estates. For pastime she took over the management of that estate. She became interested in her tenants in a warmhearted way. If they were hungry, they must be fed; if cold, they must be clothed; if sick or in trouble, they must be comforted.

On the death of her father when she was thirty-three, she moved to Eastnor Castle, where she spent seven years "in unbroken monotony," for her son was away at school. Then suddenly a new friend opened the door to a new world. Through the influence of the Philadelphia Quaker preacher Mrs. Hannah Whitall Smith, Lady Henry joined the British temperance movement. That was in 1887, four years before her first visit to America under the guidance of Mrs. Smith.

During the Chicago convention of 1891, Lady Henry spoke to an audience of four thousand. Her Sunday sermon at the world's convention in Boston was pronounced a great success. She was "tremendously impressed" by the conventions, she wrote her mother. In New York, she passed from the distinguished Sorosis to the city's dives, to its Chinatown of beautiful buildings and opium dens of shame; from there to Sing Sing prison, where she addressed the prisoners.

In all these experiences Frances Willard was at her side — "one woman in a million," she wrote. Two months later Miss Willard wrote her: ". . . the beauty of you is that you fill so many roles, and are so many folks — a sort of diamond edition of human nature. No one near me has ever been like you in that. You are my beautiful picture gallery and library, landscape and orchestra. 'A great hope, a sea to swim in.'" She named her friend Cosmos.

On her retirement to Reigate Priory fourteen years before,

Lady Henry had gathered about her a new circle of friends, many of them just as highborn as her old friends, possibly more intelligent than the old set. To be sure one woman smoked and took an occasional brandy and soda. But they all read and had something worth-while to discuss. Many were notables in their fields, whether literature, art, religion or Parliament. The circle had grown during the years, and when it widened to admit the American guest, life grew bigger and richer than ever before for Frances Willard.

At Eastnor Castle Lady Henry had thrown herself with enthusiasm into looking after her extensive estates. Warmhearted and intelligent, she could not fail to perceive how drab were the lives of the women, how prevalent was drunkenness among both men and women. Convinced that these conditions were due to "beastly" housing, she had set about rebuilding insanitary cottages. She had created model villages among the Surrey hills, where inebriate and fallen women could have medical and spiritual care, and where children from the poorhouse could develop into normal, respectable citizens.

There being no nonsense about her, she decided that, if she was to urge others to take the pledge, it was only fair that she take it herself. And take it she did, signing in the great hall of the castle, in the presence of her tenants and dependents. Finally — regretfully, wistfully, laughingly — she renounced the comforting cigarette for a like reason.

One of her intimate friends, the novelist E. F. Benson, son of the then Archbishop of Canterbury, in *As We Were* pictures her with all her "patrician charm" and the "touch of melodrama" which was an inheritance from her French ancestors. Benson liked her practical religion, her "radium-like energy." He liked, too, her public addresses, "humorous, incisive, convincing; her voice of gold." But it was her common sense, her naturalness, and her ready laugh that made her the force she was.

Such, then, was the comrade Frances Willard had found in her hour of direst need, to have and to hold these last precious years of her life. And what a to-do this friendship stirred up! Jealousies on both sides of the ocean. On Lady Henry's return from America in 1891, she had found the majority of her Temperance Association arrayed against her because of her American ideas, such as woman suffrage, opposition to the traffic in opium, championship of social purity. No mother could bring her daughter to a meeting where such themes were discussed. The most conservative said, "Lady Henry's heart is with her American friends," and they warned against "betrayal of our association into their ambushed ranks." In the end Lady Henry won reelection as their president, but thereupon the defeated party "swept from the room" and withdrew from the association. It was but a few months before the American leader came to the assistance of the British leader. Together they traveled in the interest of the W.C.T.U.

She said she detested walking, this woman who had been raised on a farm. When pleading for dress reform, she assured her audience that she would gladly walk, if there were not so many "intricate preliminaries" required of a woman. A man had but two things to do — put on his coat and crowd a hat down over his eyes. As for her, she must discard the easy wrapper in which she worked for a street dress with long, heavy skirt; she must substitute high buttoned boots for slippers. "A bonnet affording no protection from wind, light, or observation must be 'tastefully' put on"; tight-fitting gloves must be pulled into place. "Then only may the walk begin, cumbered with skirts that have to be lifted until one's knees grow weary." All these "burdens and constrictions" were so hard to endure that she was usually too tired even to get ready to take a walk.

When, therefore, in 1894, her English physician prescribed

living outdoors, she fell to musing. She detested walking; driving was not real exercise; horseback-riding was too expensive. In the end, her thoughts turned to the bicycle. That was within her means. She would learn to ride it! Three good reasons presented themselves — pure love of adventure, the zest of acquiring "a new implement of power," and last (but by no means least) to prove to herself and others that she was not too old, even at fifty-five, to become skilled in a new sport.

In less than two days of actual practice, she made herself master of what seemed to her the most ingenious and inspiring motor ever yet devised. She was too early for the automobile, but it is not at all unlikely she would have been one of the first to buy and drive a Ford "Lizzie."

Characteristically she tied the bicycle into her scheme of things. She noted the good-fellowship and mutual understanding between men and women who took the road together, singly or on the "bicycle built for two." The more interests in common, the happier the home. She blessed heaven, too, for this way of having an intoxicatingly good time without resort to alcohol.

It was long before she could persuade Lady Henry to join her. But that done, what enjoyment they had riding across country together! Together they pedaled to Duxhurst, one of Lady Henry's villages among the hills. The pretty gray cottages, the children's "Nest," the chapel, the hospital, the manor house, and Hope Hall for fallen women, all aroused Miss Willard's enthusiasm. Girls, boys, and patients furnished the music, Canon Wilberforce the address. Tea was served, while martial songs were sung lustily by crippled and blind boys. Here was religion in action — Miss Willard's kind. She would have been still more thrilled could she have known that some day her friend would leave forever the luxurious life of Eastnor

Castle (for which she really cared so little) and, dressed like a " blooming nun," says Benson, would become matron of the village.

Together they campaigned on wheels for Sir Wilfrid Laurier, liberal and teetotaler. Never had Miss Willard addressed audiences so much to her liking. She enjoyed their enthusiasm, their rising with three hearty cheers when a popular speaker came forward, their cry of " Hear! Hear! " when he scored a point. It was certainly more inspiring to the speaker than the comparatively silent audiences in America. The elections seemed more " homelike " than at home, women everywhere, even at the bars, which remained open!

Together they visited the Salvation Army, whose oddities attracted the American. The brass band, the women's quaint bonnets, the men's Garibaldi shirts gave picturesqueness. Seated on the platform, she studied bluff General Booth, noted his well poised head, his keen dark eyes, his " eagle beak like the Duke of Wellington's, his long gray beard worthy of St. Jerome." Rough men weeping at the altar recalled old-time camp meetings, but the cry, " Thirty-four in the gospel net! " (meaning the penitents) was startlingly new. Strange as the gathering seemed to her, it warmed her spirit. Not far ahead was a time when the Salvation Army would be her chief ally — and Lady Henry's — in a great crisis.

A part of their time was spent at the castle, in the luxurious mode to which Lady Henry had been accustomed before she became a reformer. One of Miss Willard's many letters to the *Union Signal* speaks of how this luxury complicated their daily routine. Take meals for example: coffee in bed with newspapers and mail, breakfast at ten, lunch at two, tea at five, and dinner at eight or nine. What more demoralizing than a day so torn to fragments! For milady there were conferences with the manager of the estate, the butler, the steward, the gardener, the heads of her charitable institutions. She must arrange almost daily outings of groups at Reigate. It was a wonder that even with half a dozen stenographers and an able secretary she could find time for temperance work. But she did. Friends feared her health would break under the strain.

"I have not written," the letter continues, "of the house parties of celebrities with their servants, of lecture trips, committee meetings, bazaar openings, of which she is the central figure." But always after the ceremonious dinner, and coffee in the Holbein Hall, there was the relaxation of bright conversation, often with guests of note, when Lady Henry's "musical voice, sparkling wit, knowledge of statecraft," were Miss Willard's constant delight.

One can but wonder, after reading these letters, what were the changes wrought in the American leader by those years with Lady Henry. The last six years of her life she spent much of her time in an environment broader than any she had known before. Changes there must have been in viewpoints, in culture, in a warmer humanism, a wider tolerance. American white-ribboners noticed the change. Some rejoiced; others murmured that she was being alienated from her own country. They failed to understand that the president of a world-wide organization should be a citizen of the world. They underestimated the work their president and Lady Henry were doing to strengthen the world movement for temperance. Perhaps those humorous letters to the *Union Signal* had misled them into thinking that their president's life in England savored too much of Elizabethan ruffs and easychairs.

(XV)

An International Figure

THREE YEARS PASSED. BUSY YEARS THEY WERE, AS HEALTH returned to the head of the temperance movement. After 1893, she missed no annual convention of the National W.C.T.U.

In 1894 she was given a public reception in New York, a demonstration so hearty as to leave no doubt she was still adored by a large following. Touched by it, she exclaimed, "*These* are my folks; *this* is my home!" The great surprise of the evening was a telegram announcing that Ohio Wesleyan University had that day conferred on her an unusual honor (for a woman), the degree of Doctor of Laws.

Manifest as it was that this meeting was a personal tribute of affection, she refused to accept it as for herself alone. She was "but the buoy held up by the sea, the windmill showing the course of the wind." Sea and wind were "the capable, self-sacrificing rank and file" of white-ribboners. To them she spoke her appreciation; with them she shared her honors.

Doubtless she heard that year of the opening of Chicago's fourth social settlement. Hull House had been opened in 1889 by Jane Addams and Ellen Starr, in a neighborhood of "filthy and rotten tenements." Two years later Charles Zeublin had begun his work as a sociologist with a practical experiment in community life, the Northwestern University Settlement. In 1893, Mary McDowell, one of Miss Willard's girls, had started the University of Chicago Settlement "behind the yards." Now, in 1894, Graham Taylor of Chicago Theological Seminary had seen something bigger than the abstractions of theology, and

Chicago Commons had been born. This was the kind of religion Frances Willard saw as the only hope of the church, the religion of hand and heart rather than of knees. She said, "If there is a place nearer heaven than one of these settlements, I have not yet found it."

After her long rest, her head was buzzing with new ideas. But first she must check the attacks from the floor of the convention on Frances Folsom Cleveland. It seems that the President's wife had christened a battleship with wine, though Missouri women had sent for the purpose water from the Mississippi and Philadelphians a beautiful bottle to hold it. Some of the attacks were sharp. But Miss Willard as peacemaker reminded the delegates that Mrs. Cleveland had proved her sincerity as a total abstainer in the difficult role of President's wife. Now she had but followed an age-old custom in such ceremonies. The Willard tolerance again brought harmony.

Two things she strongly opposed that year were lynching (which had aroused British wrath) and costly armories for reserve troops. And again she forged ahead of her time in the public reforms she advocated: police-women, amusements provided by government, compulsory arbitration in labor disputes, nationalization of transportation and communication, and signatures to editorials. Two of these have been adopted; a third is coming into operation. Most radical of all was public ownership of newspapers, to insure truth "undoctored" and news instead of propaganda. She urged that reformers buy newspaper space, and make direct appeal to the public, thereby presenting their case unbiased by prejudice. "As a man readeth in his newspaper, so is he," she paraphrased. Yet news is so twisted as to "manufacture" opinion "just as scientifically as cloth is woven."

She was reelected, but not till after those who disapproved of her long absences in England had slipped through an amendment to the by-laws obliging the president to preside at "all meetings of the body and at all executive committee meetings." *Now* would she take the hint and stay home?

In 1895, the Chicago *Tribune,* onetime hostile critic of the W.C.T.U., was unusually generous in giving space to the convention at Baltimore, from the singing of "Welcome, Chief, Welcome!" with clapping of hands and flutter of handkerchiefs, to the rather ominous ending. "Miss Willard the Star," its headline read. She looked "hearty and happy." Her address was often interrupted by laughter and applause. The mention of Lady Henry Somerset evoked a storm of applause, news of which must have cheered that lady in the nervous breakdown her friends had foreseen.

The reporter noted that many of the delegates at this convention were young. "How do you account for it?" he asked one of them.

"Easily," was her answer. "The W.C.T.U. has grown practical in its views and gained the respectful consideration of men. . . . Young women, no matter how piously inclined, have a natural dislike for anything within the ban of men's ridicule and disapproval. But now . . . young women are glad to join."

The president's address was practical. The Presbyterian General Assembly had adopted nonalcoholic communion wine. The Methodists had voted to admit women delegates to the General Conference. In acknowledging the cordial greetings given her the country over by priests and rabbis, she turned aside objections to inviting Catholic and Jewish women to membership in the Union; and following a resolution to that effect, she gave them hearty welcome.

She brought word from London that at the third biennial convention the World's Union had seated two hundred and sixty-nine delegates. The Lord Mayor had given them a formal reception, and Lady Henry Somerset had received them at Reigate Priory. Two hundred London pulpits had been filled by W.C.T.U. speakers on Sunday. The Polyglot Petition, now grown to the ponderous weight of 1730 pounds, had been displayed in Prince Albert Hall.

No one was surprised that she repeated her protest against the tyranny of dress and the exploitation of women in order to increase the sales of silk, wool and cotton. With tightly laced corsets, false hair, skirts sweeping up microbes and filth, women were to be pitied. She pleaded again for the underpaid, underfed, undersheltered wage-earner. If he could keep sober under such conditions, she declared, he deserved far more credit than the well paid and comfortable teetotaler.

But however strong the reign of common sense, however hearty the applause for their president, it could not be concealed that the dragon of dissension had reared his ugly head. And expertly as Miss Willard lopped it off, no one doubted he would grow another before the next convention.

In 1896 came the supreme test of Frances Willard's "religion in action." The year before, two Armenians had come to the convention to plead for their people, who were being raided by the Turks. To the majority of the convention Armenia had been hitherto but a name, a spot on the map. Now they were to know it as the home of a million souls bound to them by a common religion — Christians long before Europe was Christianized. Again and again their little country, site of Mount Ararat, had won independence from one conqueror only to be subjugated by another. Assyria, Persia, Greece, Rome, Turkey — each in turn an oppressor.

Now the age-old persecution had culminated in massacres that shocked the world. The reason given was the refusal of the Armenians to renounce Christianity for Mohammedanism. Their villages were burned, their crops confiscated, their women enslaved. Untold horrors were inflicted. Fifty thousand perished in one year.

When in 1896 some refugees reached Marseilles, the French government was embarrassed, lest the incident lead to international complications. The news reached England just as Lady Henry and Miss Willard were setting out on a bicycle tour of Normandy. Immediately they changed their plans. They communicated with General Booth, then went at once to Marseilles, taking with them a recent missionary to Turkey. After surveying the situation, they notified General Booth what was needed.

They found an old hospital fallen into disuse, which the city was willing to turn over to them. They had cleaned it up when a Salvation Army officer arrived with supplies. A cooperative community was established. Young men scrubbed the floors; women cut and made clothing; those who could cobbled shoes. Employment agencies were installed in several countries, to relieve the congestion in France. Two hundred of the refugees were sent to America, one hundred to England, two hundred more scattered over the Continent. The Salvation Army formally took over the hospital.

Miss Gordon thinks Miss Willard never showed more cool level-headedness and executive ability under fire of criticism than at this time, in "quiet judgment as to what could be accomplished and the choice of means to an end." In obedience to her "field order," the W.C.T.U. in America appealed to Congress to take action with Great Britain to end the atrocities. Locals organized meetings to raise funds, the clergy set aside a Sunday to arouse sympathy, money was freely donated, and a million signed the petition to Congress. Clara Barton sailed for Turkey under protection of the Red Cross with seed, food and clothing, "hope and help for all whom hope and help could reach." So began a work that lasted years.

Pathetic stories are told of the adoration among the refugees for Miss Willard. One is of a young immigrant who, when his people were met in New York harbor, took the woman's hand outstretched in greeting and bending low to kiss it murmured "Willard!" It was his only English word.

After the work was organized, there followed days of utter weariness, when she wrote: "'We shall fail you some day,' whisper tired bones and muscles as we sit together in the twilight. 'You cannot count on me as once you did,' speaks the hardest-worked muscle of all, the heart, with its emphatic beat. And then one sighs a little, until clear voices say, 'But we will never fail you — reason, hope, love — unwearied will.'"

It was that unwearied will that carried her back to America for the St. Louis convention. She had been asked to go to Jerusalem, says Miss Gordon, and invite the patriarch, whom the sultan had dismissed, to come to England with his story. Another plan had been to send her to Cyprus, to help found a colony for women and children. But she felt that in America she could do more to help Armenia.

The convention over, she spent the winter in a sanitarium at Castile, New York, where snow-clad hills and sheltering evergreens satisfied her love of beauty, while her worn-out body took on new strength. Here Susan B. Anthony came to visit her.

Miss Gordon met the guest at the railway station, and Miss Willard was waiting at the house-door to help her out of the carriage, for Miss Anthony was nearly twenty years her senior. To their delight, their guest's seventy-seven years seemed to weigh on her not at all as she dismounted with traveling-bag and umbrella. Her movements were as agile, her smile as cheery as thirty years before. They talked till the afternoon of the next day, "each," says Miss Gordon, "getting in a word as opportunity offered, and very likely saying to herself, 'There, she has stopped for a breath; now comes my chance!'"

As spring advanced, the strength Miss Willard had stored up "ebbed" away. They went to Atlantic City, where she lived outdoors in a wheel chair. But the urge of correspondence kept her dictating. Kate Jackson, on the way to Germany, stopped to see her. And, strangely enough, that last meeting took place not far from the Jackson farm, whence they had set out thirty years before for Europe, Asia, and Africa.

There followed a brief visit with Mrs. Frederick Douglas in Washington, a long deferred speaking engagement, and then some happy months with Miss Longfellow. "How little I thought," she wrote, "when a child on a Wisconsin farm, that 'Laughing Allegra' would ever lend me her pony!"

After that they pilgrimaged to the homes of her ancestors, as if to fortify her soul and round out her life. She and her mother had made the same tour when Madam Willard was seventy-five. First to Dublin, where her grandfather Willard had preached forty years; then to the Vermont hills, where Josiah Willard and Mary Thompson Hill had met and wed, and where Frances now spoke surrounded by "home-folks."

After a month in Maine and two conventions she completed the pilgrimage with a visit to Churchville, to spend Sunday with Aunt Sarah Hill, her sole surviving relative there. Then she and Anna Gordon moved westward, to Oberlin, and home.

"It will be yours to wrestle, not to reign," Madam Willard had warned. Now, after twenty years of reigning, the wrestling was to begin when, broken in health by the Armenian campaign, she had little to sustain her but faith in herself, charity for others, and that "unwearied will."

In 1897 the World's W.C.T.U. held its fourth biennial convention in Toronto. Miss Willard was greeted heartily, and everything was harmonious till someone attacked Lady Henry Somerset for lending her influence to an act to regulate social hygiene in the British army in India. The issue was between regulation and prevention — between condoning and stamping out vice. Doubtless, those raising the issue felt this was a test of their president also. How would she square her friend's action with the stand she and the Union had taken in favor of prevention of vice?

She made no attempt to square it. She said flatly that she and Lady Henry sought the same end, but differed as to the means. In the latter's absence through illness, she explained that what Lady Henry sought was "a quarantine against a contagious disease, not a license system." No one, said she hotly, could think for a moment that the English reformer desired to make vice easy. She repudiated any such charge against a woman who had braved dangerous situations in her war on vice. Peace was restored by abolishing the office of honorary vice-president. Lady Henry, out of office, was no longer a bone of contention.

Their opponents, however, were not yet through with these two friends. Someone intimated that the reason for Miss Willard's loss of interest in her American work was that she was dancing attendance on Lady Henry to the tune of five thousand dollars a year. Could it be, then, that anyone knew her and her record so little as to doubt her *integrity?* Even the press, when it ridiculed her cause and branded her followers as fanatics and office-seekers, had spared her personally, recognizing her always as sincere and unselfish in her aims. And now one of her own " sisters " dared to charge her with graft and treason! She " indignantly rebuked " her accuser. She did not deny that Lady Henry had done much for her — much that was of far more worth than money — but she did deny being in any sense a pensioner.

Two weeks later, at the national convention in Buffalo, there was another great battle to be fought, that concerning the Temple. In her autobiography Miss Willard had spoken of Mrs. Matilda B. Carse of Chicago as " one of my best and brightest coadjutors from the first." Mrs. Carse's earliest money-raising venture had been getting a hundred businessmen to contribute ten dollars each to support Miss Willard after her " blissful episode " of living by faith. In subsequent years, Mrs. Carse had financed many philanthropies: the Foundlings' Home, the W.C.T.U. Lodging House for men, its Anchorage Mission for women, its gospel meetings, free kindergartens and temperance restaurant. In 1889, she was still raising money for the Woman's Temple in Chicago, now ready to house the Union and its Publication Association. Mrs. Carse had estimated, and sound businessmen had assented, that the rentals should yield, over and above expenses, a hundred thousand dollars annually, which would go far toward financing the Union. All she had asked of the Union was its moral support and its help in selling bonds.

A magnificent plan and generous. In the light of what she had already achieved, the Union had believed she could carry it through. She might have done so, had it not been for another panic, one of the country's major depressions. Real-estate values shrank, bonds were unmarketable. The Union and its publishers were snugly housed, but other offices stood vacant. So this Temple, worthy of its name and of its famous architects, Burnham and Root, had become, like many other buildings, a liability instead of an asset. Cautious white-ribboners counseled leaving the sinking ship. Why exhaust the energies of members in raising for this purpose money that was needed to advance their reforms?

By 1895 the press had got wind of the controversy. While they gave friendly accounts of convention proceedings, reporters had warned that " Mrs. Carse and her Temple " were coming under fire. For two years the storm had been gathering. Would it break? The reporters thought it would. They did not yet know Miss Willard's resources. She had no intention of leaving her old friend, to whom the Union owed so much past service, " holding the bag." With the skill of a tactician and the heroism of a general, she had deflected the lightning to herself.

She knew of another cause of dissatisfaction — herself. Some thought she was away from home too much and neglectful of duties in her own country. Gently she reminded the delegates that with each promotion received at their hands she had had to relinquish some of her former duties. They had made her president of the World's W.C.T.U. when it was a small affair; now it had grown to be a " mighty power." In its interest she had spent parts of three years abroad. For months, as they knew, ill health had prevented her working as she had once done. Even so, given double the number of stenographers she could have had at home, she had accomplished vastly more than would have been possible in Chicago.

She had begged the convention to give thoughtful consideration to the choice of officers, especially of president. When she had been reelected unanimously, she could not restrain tears dimming her glasses as she thanked the delegates for their confidence.

Now, at the national convention of 1897 at Buffalo, she faced the crisis. Even before the convention opened, the press forecast "the Temple fight." The question must be settled whether the Union should devote its energies to saving the Temple, or turn the money it could raise into furthering the reforms for which it had been created. Mrs. Rounds, Mrs. Leavitt and other old war-horses were prepared to oppose stoutly giving even "moral" support to the Temple. They quoted a former president of the Chicago board of trade as warning they were pouring water into a sieve. Those supporting the Temple quoted a leading Chicago banker as saying the investment should pay. As for Miss Willard, her faith in and loyalty to her friend and financial backer for more than twenty years had never shone brighter.

The first day was one of routine business, but there was a tenseness that foreboded trouble. Throughout a sleepless night the president faced the situation. By morning she knew that she, and she alone, could save her friend and the Temple that was to them so much more than a building.

It was the day of her annual address. That was the deadline, beyond which lay salvation or disaster. Not till near the end of her speech, when suspense was keyed high, did she startle her listeners with the simple statement: "*I stand for the Temple.*" That meant she would be responsible for raising the three hundred thousand dollars necessary to assure control of the building. Never yet, as they knew, had she failed to raise what she had set out to raise. But three hundred thousand dollars!

"That settles it!" said the leader of the opposition.

"The jig's up!" said another.

Thereupon all the delegates pledged their cooperation, but not without a reminder from Mrs. Rounds of what the money would do in furthering their work if applied directly; not without a spiteful suggestion from another that they take Miss Willard at her word, make her honorary president, and elect a businesswoman to succeed her.

More than thirty years later, Henry Justin Smith summed up the story thus: "Like many another builder, Miss Willard found her unsolved problem in an actual building — the Temple. It was built, and it was beautiful, but it involved debt. The Temple bonds . . . brought sleepless nights to the heroic lady. After she died, the W.C.T.U. speedily voted to give up the building. . . . Today its very stones are gone."

Strong in her own integrity, and in that of her friends, Lady Henry and Mrs. Carse; uplifted by the thought of crucial fires she must pass through before that three hundred thousand dollars was raised, she went home to Evanston "invigorated," says Miss Gordon. On the way, she stopped again in Churchville, and in her birthroom recalled her mother's hope that this child would live for humanity.

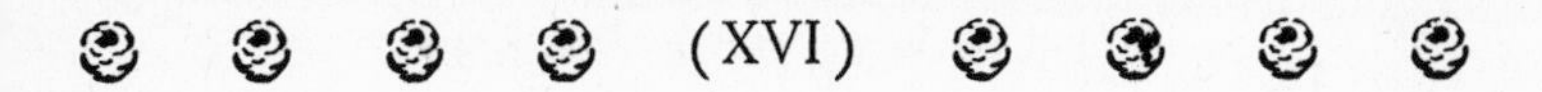

Journey's End

INVIGORATED STILL, SHE RETURNED TO EVANSTON. SHE HAD SAID, "When I reach heaven, I want to register as from Evanston." She stayed with relatives in Chicago while Rest Cottage was being set to rights — Rest Cottage filled with memories of the mother who had bidden her "enter every open door." She addressed a meeting of Northwestern and University of Chicago students. For Thanksgiving she joined a family party at the Nortons'. James Norton was her favorite cousin and son of Minerva Brace Norton, with whom she had collaborated on *A Great Mother*. There was another family gathering at Christmas. On New Year's day she spoke at Janesville to an audience in which were a few friends of her childhood. She spent a day at Forest Home and the schoolhouse near by.

Now all the good-bys had been said. One cannot doubt she knew they were final. The brief exhilaration at the conventions, the invigoration following them, had been deceptive. Though at fifty-nine one is not to be thought of as old, her marvelous energy was exhausted. She was tired — so tired. She said so again and again.

Manager Quinn, of the Hotel Empire, New York, placed a suite at her disposal. Here she settled down with Miss Gordon and a stenographer, "to work." Serenely they adjusted themselves to the old routine of correspondence, articles, dates for conferences and addresses. A month passed. Gradually the hours of work grew shorter. Then they stopped altogether.

Doctors and a nurse took charge. "Grippe," was the diagnosis. She who had been a famous sleeper could sleep no more. Anna Gordon soothed her with her favorite poems and hymns, singing at all hours of the night.

Letters, telegrams, flowers attested the love and concern of friends. Mrs. L. M. N. Stevens, Miss Willard's logical successor, was summoned. The sick woman smiled her welcome and whispered, " I was sure you would come, Stevie."

A few more days, then journey's end. She knew now it was near. Yet almost to the last she would say, " Could I dictate just one very important letter? " Her constant injunction was not to forget this or that. Once she mused, " We white-ribboners have had a great and beautiful past, and people don't know it. They think we are fanatics." And again, " We have fought amidst great ostracism."

Her niece Katharine brought lilies of the valley — " grandma's flowers " — for her to hold. Messages were sent to Mary B. Willard and Mamie in Berlin, and to many old friends. As the exhaustion of approaching death became almost unbearable, she mustered her old whimsicalness and said with a smile: " ' He giveth His beloved sleep '; but sometimes he's a long time doing it. . . . He has other worlds, and I want to go! " And drowsily " ' I am Merlin and I follow the gleam.' . . . How beautiful it is to be with God."

So she adventured forth, quietly, gently, as she had lived, still following the gleam.

At once friends began gathering, till the hotel parlors were filled. Later they gathered at the Broadway Tabernacle for a simple service, where Mary Lowe Dickinson spoke for them all when she said, " We know no woman whose homecoming would have left so many other women feeling as if the sun had gone." Many who had attended the last world convention at Toronto recalled her as she had stood transfigured against the background of a thousand children in chorus, waving glad welcome to the woman who looked more of heaven than of earth.

The flower-covered casket was placed in a special car, and made its slow progress westward. It stopped at Churchville, where she had so lately been, and at Buffalo, where flags hung at half-mast all day and Bishop Vincent conducted an impressive service.

In Willard Hall of the Woman's Temple her body lay in state. "Of all the tributes paid Frances E. Willard during her gentle life," said the *Daily News,* "none was greater than that paid her in death, when thousands of women braved the storm to stand in line for hours at the Temple, to look once more upon her face." It is said that more than thirty thousand men, women and children passed the casket for that last look.

The saying about a prophet in his own country was not verified in the case of Miss Willard. Editorials in the papers of her own city gave her praise, spoke with pride of her fame and with love of her "gentle" self. The *Tribune* saw in her a typical American woman of the period, with genius developed by culture. The *Post* thought it would be difficult to overestimate her influence and that of her Union.

The *News* dwelt on her success as a harmonizer. She was never partisan, "never lost her mental equilibrium, never forgot the single aim involved." The world had been warned against people of a single idea, but it had never been thought dangerous to possess a single purpose. "Miss Willard," said the editor, "was full to overflowing of ideas, but she had a single intent, and that was to bring sobriety, purity and character into every heart and home in the whole world."

Following the private service at Rest Cottage came the thronged church, the white-draped Willard pew, the casket on a rug of roses and violets, its chief decoration a heart of white flowers from Lady Henry, whom Miss Willard was soon to have joined. Behind the pulpit was the flag made by British women to be carried at the World's Fair in Chicago in 1893. Since then it had traveled from convention to convention, four thousand miles in all. It had hung above Miss Willard living; it drooped near her body in farewell. From the organ-loft floated the Stars and Stripes. And overarching all was a rainbow of spring flowers, a bow of promise, within which hung her last words, "How beautiful it is to be with God!"

The long processional moves slowly down the aisle, led by Dr. Frank M. Bristol, once her student, now her pastor. He is followed by the president and faculty of Northwestern University, the officers of the W.C.T.U., and two relatives, Katharine Willard Baldwin and her brother Robert Willard. To emphasize Miss Willard's connection with the university, first as dean, then as trustee, the pallbearers are university students, and most of the speakers are professors. The W.C.T.U.'s tribute is paid by Mrs. Louise S. Rounds, whose letter in 1874 persuaded Miss Willard to enter the temperance movement. For twenty-three years she staunchly supported her chosen leader. If recently, in the Temple fight, they led opposing forces, it did not spoil their friendship..

Others speak. Last of all Dr. Bristol voices what he calls "her message to us all." "The holy place," said he, "is not in the sanctuary or on the mountain, in the cell of the monastery, in the sweet quiet of ease and culture, . . . but in the life of humanity, in the midst of the world's sorrow, and wrongs, and struggles, in the center of society, in the great heart of the age. From that holy place alone can man or woman pray to be heard, worship to be accepted, believe to be saved."

Rosehill's receiving vault was blanketed in snow, fit setting for the resting place of a white-ribboner's ashes. Even in death

Frances Willard led a new cause. "Let no friend of mine," she had said, "say aught to prevent the cremation of my cast-off body." So in the crematory, converted into a bower of flowers, relatives gathered to watch the novel ceremony. The casket slid through the doorway of the furnace, where the beautiful body, no longer needed, was turned to a handful of ashes and stored in a snow-white box to await the spring.

When April filled the air and birds began to sing, Madam Willard's grave was opened and lined with evergreens from ancestral homes. Then Frances Willard's ashes were strewn upon her mother's casket. "For the things that are seen are temporal, but the things that are unseen are eternal," sounded the words of the Book by which she had guided her steps.

FRANCES WILLARD'S WILL

This is my last Will and Testament after fifty-six years of my Heavenly Father's discipline and blessing to prepare me for better work hereafter (as I believe) in wonderful worlds unknown.

All of my personal property and the summer homes at Twilight Park, Catskill Mts., N. Y., Pacific Coast Chautauqua near Astoria, Oregon, and near Bar Harbor, Maine (Willard's Acre), of all of which I have deeds, I bequeath to my beloved Anna Gordon, who is to have them out and out and forever.

The Rest Cottage home at Evanston, Ill., (deed recorded in Chicago) I bequeath to my beloved sister, Mary Bannister Willard and to Anna Gordon equally, to be used by them or dealt with as they deem best during their lifetime, and to be made available to either or both of my nieces, Katharine Willard Baldwin and Mary Willard, if they should have need thereof, but to revert aside from the claimants herein named to the Women's Christian Temperance Union for the purpose of teaching boys and girls the evil effects of alcoholics and tobacco upon the tissues of the body and temper of the soul and to indoctrinate them in habits of personal purity in word and deed. (This disposition of the dear old home is in accordance with the understanding I had with my blessed mother, who hallowed it by so much of her life, and by her triumphal passage to Heaven from within its peaceful walls.)

Remembrances of me are to be given by Anna Gordon to my dear relatives and comrades according to her knowledge of my wishes.

My dear friend Kate Jackson is to choose whatever she would like, as souvenirs of one who knew her long and gratefully remembers her loving kindness in earlier days.

To my beloved Isabel Somerset, who has everything that heart could wish, I have nothing to leave, save that she may choose any souvenirs she likes, and the undying gratitude toward one whom my mother loved from the first hour of her coming into our lives, even as I did. I make her and Anna Gordon my literary executors and the executors of my will and testament.

In my personal property is as a matter of course included the Birthday Fund of three thousand dollars given by sister white-ribboners on my fiftieth birthday.

Signed
FRANCES E. WILLARD

Witnesses
Susanna W. D. Fry
Ada M. Melville

(XVII)

National Honors

SEVEN YEARS PASSED. ON THE SEVENTEENTH OF FEBRUARY, 1905, a thousand children marched up Pennsylvania avenue to the nation's capitol. Under the dome of the rotunda they stood in reverent admiration before a statue carved in white marble. Unlike the statues around it, it was the figure of a woman — a woman standing at ease beside a pulpit, as if she were preaching. When they had all assembled, a little woman whom many of them knew from her picture to be Miss Gordon, spoke. She thanked the men of Illinois for sending this statue of Miss Willard to stand in the capitol. For them she laid at its feet a wreath of laurel and palm, emblems of victory in life and in death.

When it came the children's turn, they passed along a lane railed off, and each child in passing the snow-white lady dropped a flower, till she stood knee-deep in blossoms. The children then went back to their schoolrooms, carrying the memory of the woman who had worked for clean living and happy homes.

Meanwhile, the lawmakers of the land suspended business for an hour to accept and dedicate this second and last statue that Illinois was entitled to place in Statuary Hall, in honor of those who had brought honor to their state.

In the Senate chamber, the venerable Edward Everett Hale opened the ceremony with Scripture and prayer. A letter from Governor Deneen of Illinois, presenting the statue, was read. Then Illinois' two senators spoke. Senator Cullom declared that Miss Willard was that extraordinary being, "a popular reformer." Senator Hopkins recalled what she had achieved despite " envious tongues and detractors " and the " sharp thrusts of critics." Senator Dolliver of Iowa called her " a teacher of social and moral science." Senator Beveridge of Indiana explained her fight for better homes by that isolation in childhood that had made home the center of all her activities.

In the House spoke five Representatives: Foss, Rainey, and Graff of Illinois, Littlefield of Maine, and Brooks of Colorado. To Mr. Littlefield the secret of her success lay in " her attractive person, her voice of marvelous sweetness and purity, her intellect, logic, persuasiveness, and eloquence."

No tribute would have pleased her more than that of Mr. Brooks: " Mr. Speaker," he began, " Colorado owes much to Illinois. From her we derived our form of state constitution; from her also we took many of our statute laws; from her came many of the pioneers who helped to give form and shape to the state's new life. But no debt of Colorado to her mother state exceeds in importance that which she owes for the precious memory of Frances Willard. . . . Her life has not been without its definite, tangible, present results in that state at least. Much that she labored for has there been achieved.

" Colorado," he continued, " is one of the four states of the Union which have accorded to women full civic rights, which recognize in fullest measure her equality before the law on a plane in all respects equal to that occupied by her brothers. . . . In every line of civic activities, that commonwealth has received and has appreciated the benefit of women's counsels, help, and active constructive work. . . . In the lives and homes of her people [Colorado] will perpetuate and cherish the memory of Frances Willard."

Senator Beveridge had called her " the most beloved character of her time." She had often been called in simpler speech " the best-loved woman in America." Admiring the settlement idea as she did, she would have been glad that her successor to the title would be Jane Addams.

On University Heights in New York City stands the Hall of Fame for Great Americans, built by the bequest of Helen Gould Shepard. Within its granite colonnade are one hundred and fifty panels for one hundred and fifty bronze tablets to Americans, native or foreign-born, whom the committee of one hundred notables deem worthy of such honor.

To this Hall of Fame Frances Elizabeth Willard was admitted in 1910. Entering at the same time were Harriet Beecher Stowe, Oliver Wendell Holmes, Edgar Allan Poe, William Cullen Bryant, Phillips Brooks, Roger Williams, George Bancroft, and John Lothrop Motley. Some of them had waited far longer than she for the honor. Above the tablet is her bust, the seventh of famous American women representative of different spheres of action: actress, Charlotte Cushman; author, Harriet Beecher Stowe; scientist, Maria Mitchell; educators, Mary Lyon, Emma Willard, and Alice Freeman Palmer. Frances E. Willard is enrolled as "social worker" — a name she would have much preferred to "reformer." It draws her closer to humanity. It substitutes for the sword of the crusader the white ribbon of service.

CHRONOLOGY

1634 Major Simon Willard, of Kent, England, settles in Concord, Mass. Descendants: Two presidents of Harvard; Samuel, pastor of Old South Church, Boston, opposed to burning witches; Solomon, designer of Bunker Hill Monument.

1735 Born — Oliver A. Willard, Frances' grandfather.

1775 Nathaniel Thompson in danger for toasting Washington.

1805 Born — Josiah Flint Willard and Mary Thompson Hill (Willard).

1839 Born — Frances Elizabeth Willard at Churchville, N. Y., Sept. 28.

1841 Willards move to Oberlin, where Josiah builds home.

1846 They move to Wisconsin farm, Forest Home, six miles from Janesville. Josiah in Wisconsin legislature for several years.

1851–55 Frances and Mary taught by mother; by Miss Burdick two summers; in little schoolhouse. Study music at state Institute for the Blind.

1852 Oliver enters Beloit College.

1855 Oliver casts first vote. Frances at sixteen " settles down." She has shown ability as organizer in Fort City and in clubs. Uncle Zophar and aunts come from East to visit. Mrs. Willard returns with them. She goes a second time. Mr. Willard takes girls East. Willards meet Whitmans of Georgia in Janesville, girls study with Whitmans for six weeks. Frances begins French and reads first novel. Melodeon gives way to piano.

1857 Spring — Girls enter Milwaukee Female College.

1858 March — Girls enter Northwestern Female College, Evanston, Ill. Summer — Frances teaches in Forest Home schoolhouse. Dec. — Mr. and Mrs. Willard become Evanstonians.

1859 Frances graduates from Northwestern Female College. Teaches at Harlem.

1860 Frances teaches at Kankakee; at Harlem again. Is engaged.

1861 Hears a lecture on temperance. She and Mary join church. Frances teaches in Evanston with Mary Bannister.

1862 Mary dies. Oliver and Mary Bannister marry and move to

Denver. Swampscott closed, Forest Home sold. Mrs. Willard goes East. Frances teaches science at alma mater.

1863 Teaches at Pittsburgh Female College.

1863–65 Temperance Alliance active in Evanston.

1865–66 Frances teaches in Grove School, Evanston. Intimacy with Kate Jackson begins. Willards build and move into Rest Cottage. Frances secretary of Methodist Ladies' Centenary Association.

1866–67 She and Kate Jackson teach at Genessee Wesleyan Seminary.

1868 Mr. Willard dies at Churchville, N. Y.

1868–70 Frances and Kate travel in Europe, Asia and Africa. Mr. Jackson dies (1869). Kate one of Willard family in 1870.

1871 Sept. — Evanston College for Ladies opens, with Miss Willard president. Oct. 9 — Chicago fire ruins its financial backing. Degree of M.A. conferred on Miss Willard by Syracuse University.

1872 June — Evanston College for Ladies has first and only Commencement.

1873 Business panic ruins its plans. Northwestern University takes over its property and completes building. President Willard becomes Dean Willard in Northwestern.

1874 March — Evanston Temperance Union (later W.C.T.U.) is formed. June — Dean Willard resigns; goes East to study temperance movement. Accepts presidency of Chicago Woman's Temperance Union. Oct. — Illinois Union formed at Bloomington, Jennie F. Willing, president; Frances E. Willard, secretary. Nov. 17 — National Woman's Christian Temperance Union formed in Cleveland, O.; 17 states represented; constitution presented by J. Ellen Foster of Iowa, plan of work by F. E. Willard of Illinois; organize in 11 states. Evanston W.C.T.U. sets pattern, with Band of Hope, and Young Woman's Union led by Mary McDowell. Three Evanstonians prominent in first convention. First of many memorials to Congress grows to 40,000 names. Woman's Congress loth to hear Miss Willard on unpopular subject. Reformed Men's Club formed in Chicago.

1875 Mrs. Carse raises salary for Chicago president. Summer —

F. E. Willard writes *Hints and Helps for the W.C.T.U.* Asks to speak on home protection ballot for women; refused hearing by all but Woman's Congress. Cincinnati Convention — 17 states now organized; standing committees created; homes for inebriates urged; W.C.T.U. asks use of unfermented wine at communion. Memorial presented to Congress by Senator Morton (Ind.) dies in committee.

1876 Newark Convention — Miss Willard speaks for suffrage, is rebuked; motto chosen; Congress asked to investigate cost and results of liquor traffic; report four summer assemblies have W.C.T.U. day; Miss Willard urges industrial and evening schools. Miss Willard joins Moody.

1877 She goes with Moody to Boston. Speaks before House Judiciary Committee on home protection ballot. Declines Moody offer. Chicago Convention — adopts white ribbon badge; praises Mrs. Hayes for abolishing wine in White House; Miss Willard declines nomination for president; recommends (1) enlisting cooperation of other organizations and press; (2) distribution of temperance literature; (3) Friendly Inns; (4) interesting capital and labor in temperance; (5) teaching laws of heredity and health.

1878 Miss Willard joins Lyceum Bureau. Then free lance for W.C.T.U. Oliver Willard's death. Mary B. Willard moves to Rest Cottage. Home Protection campaign radiates from Springfield. Overwhelming victory for drys in fall elections. Baltimore Convention — Shall women ask to vote on local option?

1879 Indianapolis Convention — 148 delegates from 20 states; cleavage into conservatives and liberals; Frances Willard, liberal, made national president; immediate increase in efficiency; National Education Association enlisted as ally.

1880 Boston Convention — 177 delegates from 25 states; six departments: Preventive, Educational, Evangelistic, Social, Legal, and Organization. Mrs. Carse founds the *Signal* (in 1882 merged with *Our Union* and named *Union Signal,* Mary B. Willard editor, later Mary Allen West). Headquarters opened in New York City. W.C.T.U. gives Miss Willard cottage in

Catskills. S. M. I. Henry is training workers. Mrs. Hunt heads Education.

1881 Miss Willard presents portrait of Mrs. Hayes to White House. Finds President Garfield cool to "reforms." Organizes southern women. Sees need of "longitudinal" party. At Saratoga meets James Black.

1882 Prohibition party reorganized. Miss Willard on committee. Louisville Convention — She asks W.C.T.U. to endorse new party; no action taken; Committee on Franchise created. Work begun among soldiers and sailors. Vermont first state to adopt scientific temperance instruction. Louisa M. Alcott active as secretary of Concord W.C.T.U.

1883 Misses Willard and Gordon organize West and Southwest, cover 30,000 miles. Detroit Convention — celebrates First Decade; Union now truly "national"; spirited debate on *equal* suffrage; Foster-Willard split on political action; physicians asked to use nonalcoholic medicines. Work begun in lumber camps. New Hampshire second state to adopt temperance instruction. Idea of World's W.C.T.U. adopted; Mrs. Leavitt first "missionary." Evanston forms Law and Order League.

1884 Miss Willard on National Committee of Prohibition party; seconds nomination of St. John for President; writes suffrage plank with educational test for voters. Asks each National Committee for prohibition plank. Writes Polyglot Petition. *Century* magazine offers space for worth-while temperance article. Mary B. Willard moves to Germany, promotes German W.C.T.U. St. Louis Convention — cold-shouldered because thought to be Prohibitionist.

1885 Madam Willard celebrates eightieth birthday. Evanston opens first W.C.T.U. free kindergarten, named for Mary Bannister Willard, forms a Good Times Club and, by request of Negroes, a colored W.C.T.U. Philadelphia Convention — 282 delegates from 40 states and territories; ten more states have adopted temperance education; White Cross is organized; Margaret Bright Lucas made president of World's W.C.T.U.; Mary B. Willard presents Polyglot Petition for first time.

1886 In Evanston Good Templars open Willard Lodge to both sexes. Minneapolis Convention — authorizes Willard letter to labor bodies, in it are listed W.C.T.U. activities to date; fashion magazines asked to encourage more normal physique. Training School (later School of Methods) in operation. Nine more states have temperance education.

1887 Nashville Convention — 341 delegates from 42 states and territories; only 14 vote against supporting Prohibition party; six more states to teach temperance; Pundita Ramabai among distinguished foreign guests. New York *Christian Advocate,* hitherto opposed, asks Miss Willard to send article.

1888 Frances Willard and Susan B. Anthony found National and International Councils of Women; Miss Anthony heads International, Miss Willard heads National Council. Prohibition party convention at Indianapolis; Miss Willard forces inclusion of suffrage plank. New York W.C.T.U. Convention in Metropolitan Opera House; Mrs. Foster draws sharp rebuttals from Prohibitionists.

1889 Sept. 28 — Frances Willard's fiftieth birthday; Evanston's tribute to her. Chicago Convention — hails appearance of *Glimpses of Fifty Years;* Department of Peace and International Arbitration created; Foster faction withdraws from W.C.T.U.; celebration of birthday.

1890 Atlanta Convention — Departments of Physical Education and of Humane Education created.

1891 World's W.C.T.U. holds its first convention, in Faneuil Hall, Boston; Frances Willard, president; 50 nations organized, 17 send delegates; Lady Henry Somerset in America for first time. Its business done, the Union joins Boston Convention of National W.C.T.U.

1892 Aug. 6 — Madam Willard dies. Misses Willard and Gordon sail for England to be guests of Lady Henry Somerset. Lady Henry returns with Miss Willard for Denver Convention. Winter — British ovation to Miss Willard in Exeter Hall, London. Triumphal tour of Great Britain and Ireland with Lady Henry.

1893 World's and National W.C.T.U. welcomed at World's Columbian Exposition. Chicago Convention — Miss Willard recuperating in England; Lady Henry presides and reads president's address stressing new status of woman recognized by Exposition; foreign speakers featured.

1894 Frances Willard a bicycle "fan." She and Lady Henry wheel to meetings. New York ovation to returning president. Miss Willard made LL.D. by Ohio Wesleyan University. Cleveland Convention — Miss Willard recommends (1) policewomen; (2) amusements provided by government; (3) compulsory arbitration in labor disputes; (4) nationalization of transportation and communication; (5) signed editorials; (6) publicly owned newspapers; (7) purchase of space in newspapers to present needed reforms.

1895 World's W.C.T.U. meets in Queen's Hall, London; Polyglot Petition, displayed in Prince Albert Hall, now weighs 1730 pounds; translated into 50 tongues it is ready to send to 50 rulers; illuminated copy presented to Queen Victoria by Lady Henry. London mayor gives reception. Lady Henry receives at Priory. 200 London pulpits filled by women on convention Sunday. Baltimore Convention of National W.C.T.U. — Number of young delegates noticeable; Polyglot Petition presented to President Cleveland; Presbyterians have adopted unfermented wine; Methodists have voted to admit women delegates to General Conference; Catholics and Jews are invited to join W.C.T.U.; Woman's Temple under fire.

1896 Armenian campaign. St. Louis Convention. Miss Willard winters in sanitarium at Castile, N. Y.; visited by Susan B. Anthony.

1897 Spring — Miss Willard at Atlantic City in wheel chair; Kate Jackson comes. Pilgrimage to ancestral homes, then to Evanston. World's W.C.T.U. Convention at Toronto — 211 delegates from 39 countries; 19 departments. Buffalo Convention of National W.C.T.U. — "Mrs. Carse and her Temple" saved by checkmate; Miss Willard assumes burden of indebtedness. Home to Evanston via Churchville. Gathers relatives for Thanksgiving and Christmas. Addresses students of Northwestern and University of Chicago.

1898 New Year's day at Janesville and Forest Home. Manager Quinn invites Miss Willard and her staff to Hotel Empire,

New York. Settles down to work with Miss Gordon and stenographer. Feb. 17 — Death comes. Services in New York. Services at Churchville and Buffalo as body moves westward. Evanston's last tribute. Cremation. April — Burial of ashes at Rosehill.

1903 Forty-eighth state adopts temperance education.

1905 Willard statue placed in Statuary Hall, National Capitol.

1910 Bust and tablet placed in Hall of Fame, New York City.

FEDERAL LEGISLATION IN YEARS FOLLOWING FRANCES WILLARD'S DEATH

1901 Anti-canteen law abolishes liquor in army posts and transports.

1903 Recreation buildings substituted. Capitol building "dry."

1904 Beer halls prohibited in state and territorial soldiers' homes.

1906 Canteens in national soldiers' homes prohibited, also sales to Indians. Prohibition in Arizona. New Mexico enabling act.

1907 Prohibition zones created around government institutions.

1908 Liquor barred from mails.

1909 Liquor shipment law to protect dry territory. Antiliquor code for Alaska.

1911 Resolution for national constitutional prohibition introduced in Congress by Captain Richmond Pearson Hobson.

1911 and 1913 Appropriations for international congresses on alcoholism.

1913 Interstate liquor shipment law passed over President's veto.

1914 Hobson resolution receives majority, but not necessary two-thirds vote in House. Penalty for intemperance in army.

1917 Enforcement code for Alaska. Prohibition for Puerto Rico, for District of Columbia. Liquor advertising in mails and shipment of liquor into dry states prohibited; use of foodstuffs for making alcoholic beverages made optional with President. Aug. 1 — Senate (as elected 1912, 1914, 1916) votes 65 to 20 for Eighteenth Amendment resolution. Dec. 17 — House of Representatives (election five months before U. S. entered World War) votes for same, 282 to 128.

1918 Prohibition for Hawaii. Prohibition around coal mines and war industries.

1919 Jan. 16 — Eighteenth Amendment ratified by thirty-sixth state. By March 1, forty-five states ratify it.
1920 Jan. 16 — Prohibition becomes operative.
1933 Prohibition repealed by Twenty-first Amendment.

PROGRESS OF WOMAN SUFFRAGE

1893 Granted in New Zealand.
1895–1902 In states composing Australia.
1906 In Finland.
1907 In Norway.
1909 In Sweden.
1915 In Denmark.
1917–19 In Great Britain, Russia, Canada, Germany, Austria, Hungary, Czechoslovakia, Holland, South Africa.
1920 In United States of America (Nineteenth Amendment).
1931 In Spain.

BIBLIOGRAPHY

Abbot, Willis J. *Notable Women in History.* Winston, 1913.

Benson, E. F. Lady Henry Somerset in *As We Were.* Longmans, 1930.

Bradford, Gamaliel. *Portraits of American Women.* Houghton, 1919.

——— *Life and I.* Houghton, 1928.

Cherrington, Ernest H. *The Evolution of Prohibition in the U.S.A.* American Issue Press, 1920.

Colvin, D. Leigh. *Prohibition in the United States.* Doran, 1920.

Dibble, R. F. *Strenuous Americans.* Boni & Liveright, 1923.

Elson, Henry. *The Story of a Noble Life.* Stradling, 1899.

Fitzpatrick, Kathleen. *Lady Henry Somerset.* Little, Brown, 1923.

Flynt, Josiah (Frank Willard). *My Life.* Outing Publishing Co., 1908.

Gordon, Anna A. *The Beautiful Life of F. E. Willard.* Introduction by Lady Henry Somerset. W.C.T.U.

——— *What F. E. Willard Said.* Revell, 1907.

Gordon, Elizabeth P. *Women Torch-Bearers.* W.C.T.U.

Hurd and Sheppard. History of Evanston in *Historical Encyclopedia of Illinois.* Munsell, 1906.

Kiwanis Club. *Evanston.* 1924.

Leavitt, Gertrude S. *The Story of Frances Willard.* Nelson, 1905.

Lewis and Smith. *Chicago, The History of Its Reputation.* Harcourt, 1929.

Reeling, V. Crouch. *Evanston: Its Land,* etc. W. B. Conkey, Printer, 1928.

Stewart, Jane A. *The Frances Willard Book.* Current Syndicate, 1906.

Strachey, Ray. *Frances Willard, Her Life and Work.* Introduction by Lady Henry Somerset. Revell, 1913.

U.S.A. *Statue of Miss F. E. Willard in Statuary Hall.* Government Printing Office, 1905.

Ward, Estelle F. *The Story of Northwestern University.* Dodd, Mead, 1924.

Willard, Frances E. *A Classic Town* (Evanston). W.C.T.U., 1891.
——— *How to Win: A Book for Girls.* Funk & Wagnalls, 1886.
——— *Woman and Temperance.* W.C.T.U., 1897.
——— *Woman in the Pulpit.* W.C.T.U., 1889.
——— *Glimpses of Fifty Years* (Autobiography). Introduction by Hannah Whitall Smith. W.C.T.U., 1889.
——— *My Happy Half-Century.* Introduction by Lady Henry Somerset. Edited by F. E. Cook. Ward, Lock, London.
——— *Nineteen Beautiful Years.* Harper, 1864.
——— *A Wheel within a Wheel, or How I Learned to Ride the Bicycle.* Revell, 1896.
——— and Norton, Minerva B. *A Great Mother.* Introduction by Lady Henry Somerset. W.C.T.U., 1894.
W.C.T.U. *A Brief History of the W.C.T.U.* Union Signal Press, 1907.

JUNIOR BOOKS

Babcock, Bernie. *An Uncrowned Queen.* Revell, 1902.
Thayer, Wm. M. *Women Who Win.* Nelson, 1896.
Tinling, C. I. *Stories about Frances E. Willard.* R. James, London.

ACKNOWLEDGMENTS

The author is grateful to officers of the Woman's Christian Temperance Union for reading the manuscript of this book, for the use of its library and valuable papers, and for the illustrations herein used. She is much indebted to Mr. Charles S. Winslow, who went through magazines and newspapers from 1882 to 1898, the year of Miss Willard's death, copying all material that was relevant. She is especially happy that the Chicago *Tribune* and the Chicago *Daily News* gave such full reports of the W.C.T.U. and Prohibition party conventions during that period, thus enabling her to see these gatherings through the eyes of the public as represented by the press. To Mrs. James H. Norton's scrapbook she owes some lively articles from the Evanston *Index* and the Evanston *Press*.